First World War
and Army of Occupation
War Diary
France, Belgium and Germany

33 DIVISION
Divisional Troops
156 Brigade Royal Field Artillery
3 February 1915 - 13 June 1919

WO95/2413/3

The Naval & Military Press Ltd
www.nmarchive.com
Published in association with The National Archives

Published by

The Naval & Military Press Ltd

Unit 10 Ridgewood Industrial Park,

Uckfield, East Sussex,

TN22 5QE England

Tel: +44 (0) 1825 749494

www.naval-military-press.com

www.nmarchive.com

Contents

Document type	Place/Title	Date From	Date To
Heading	WO95/2413/3		
Heading	33rd Division Divl Artillery 156th Brigade R.F.A. Feb 1915-Apr 1919		
Heading	33 156th Bde R.F.A. Vol 4		
Heading	156th Bde R.F.A. Vol I 33rd From Formation Dec 15 April 19		
War Diary	Grove Vale East Dulwich London	03/02/1915	29/07/1915
War Diary	From Waterloo	04/08/1915	11/08/1915
War Diary	Bulford	12/08/1915	10/12/1915
War Diary	Southampton	04/12/1915	04/12/1915
War Diary	Le Havre	13/12/1915	13/12/1915
War Diary	Mazinghem	15/12/1915	19/12/1915
War Diary	Aire	19/12/1915	19/12/1915
War Diary	Mazinghem	15/12/1915	17/02/1916
Miscellaneous	156th Brigade R.F.A.		
Heading	War Diary Of 156th Bde R.F.A. From Feb1st 1916 To March 1st 1916		
War Diary	Mazinghem	04/02/1916	27/02/1916
War Diary	Bethune	28/02/1916	29/02/1916
Heading	War Diary Of 156th Bde R.F.A. From March 1st 1916 To March 31st 1916 Volume 5		
War Diary	Annequin	01/03/1916	01/03/1916
War Diary	Annequin N	01/03/1916	31/03/1916
Heading	War Diary Of 156 F.A. Bde From April 1st To April 30th Volume XXXIII		
War Diary	Annequin N	01/04/1916	30/04/1916
Miscellaneous	Appendix I Detail Of Artillery Employed		
Miscellaneous	Appendix II Lieut-Col. H. Rochfort-Boyd, D.S.O.		
Miscellaneous	Appendix III		
Heading	War Diary Of 156th Bde R.F.A. From May 1st 1916 To May 31st 1916 Volume 4		
War Diary	Annequin	02/05/1916	28/05/1916
War Diary	Annequin	01/05/1916	31/05/1916
Miscellaneous	Appendix I		
Miscellaneous	Programme Of 1st Phase. Zero Time 4 P.M		
Miscellaneous	Programme Of 1st Phase. Zero Time 10.30 P.m Repeated At 12.00 A.M. & 30 A.M.		
Miscellaneous	Cuinchy Group. R.F.A.	23/05/1916	23/05/1916
Miscellaneous	156 Bde R.F.A.		
Miscellaneous			
Miscellaneous	Appendix I Instructions For Enterprise Night Of 27/28th June 1916		
Heading	War Diary Headquarters, 156th Brigade R.F.A. (33rd Division) July 1916		
War Diary	Givenchy	01/07/1916	15/07/1916
War Diary	Mametz Wood	15/07/1916	23/07/1916
War Diary		17/07/1916	28/07/1916
War Diary		17/07/1916	31/07/1916
Miscellaneous	Appendices 1 & 2		
Miscellaneous	Appendix I Givenchy Group		

Diagram etc	Programme To A/162		
Diagram etc	Programme Of A 156		
Diagram etc	Programme for Howitzers.		
Diagram etc	Programme of C/186 Frontal Fire 4-18 Prs		
Diagram etc	Status Mortars		
Diagram etc	2nd Mortars (12) Zones O.O. To 0.45 Barrage after 0.45 Shaved		
Miscellaneous	G.O.C. 33rd Division	10/07/1916	10/07/1916
Miscellaneous	File		
Miscellaneous	Appendix 2 O.C. 156 Brigade, R.F.A.	19/07/1916	19/07/1916
Miscellaneous	Arrangements For Night Firing	19/07/1916	19/07/1916
Operation(al) Order(s)	XV Corps Artillery Operation Order No. 24	19/07/1916	19/07/1916
Operation(al) Order(s)	33rd Division Order No. 54	18/07/1916	18/07/1916
Miscellaneous	Amendments To Instructions For Bombardment And Barrages	18/07/1916	18/07/1916
Heading	33rd Divisional Artillery 156th Brigade Royal Field Artillery August 1916		
Heading	War Diary Of 156th Bde. R.F.A. From Aug 1st 1916 To Aug 31st 1916 Volume 7		
Miscellaneous			
War Diary	Bazentin Le Grand	01/08/1916	04/08/1916
War Diary	Bazentin	05/08/1916	08/08/1916
War Diary	Somme Bazentin	08/08/1916	23/08/1916
War Diary	Montauban	24/08/1916	29/08/1916
War Diary	Somme Montauban	30/08/1916	31/08/1916
Operation(al) Order(s)	Appendix I 7th Divisional Artillery Operation Order No. 27	30/08/1916	30/08/1916
Operation(al) Order(s)	Appendix 2 7th Divisional Artillery Operation Order No. 28	04/09/1916	04/09/1916
Miscellaneous			
Miscellaneous	Appendix 3 Co-Operation Of Divisional Artillery With R.F.C.		
Operation(al) Order(s)	Appendix 1 51st Divisional Artillery Operation Order No. 39	01/08/1916	01/08/1916
Operation(al) Order(s)	Appendix 2 51st Divisional Artillery Operation Order No. 41	07/08/1916	07/08/1916
Miscellaneous	War Diary		
Operation(al) Order(s)	Appendix 3 Operation Order No. 24 By Brigadier-General H.S. Seligman. Commanding R.A. 7th Division	23/08/1916	23/08/1916
Miscellaneous	Appendix 4 156th Brigade, R.F.A. Monthly Casualty Return	01/09/1916	01/09/1916
War Diary		01/09/1916	30/09/1916
Miscellaneous	156th Brigade, R.F.A. Monthly Casualty Return	30/09/1916	30/09/1916
War Diary		04/10/1916	26/10/1916
Miscellaneous	156 Brigade R.F.A. Monthly Casualty Return	31/10/1916	31/10/1916
Miscellaneous	Appendix 1 33rd D.A. No. BM/S/835		
War Diary		02/11/1916	23/11/1916
Miscellaneous			
Miscellaneous	Please Supply The Following Documents		
Operation(al) Order(s)	166 Brigade Order No. 3	06/11/1916	06/11/1916
War Diary		01/12/1916	31/12/1916
War Diary	N. Of Maurepas	05/01/1917	12/01/1917
War Diary	Camp 14	13/01/1917	20/01/1917
War Diary	Vaux Wood	21/01/1917	21/01/1917
War Diary	W. Of Clery	22/01/1917	22/01/1917

Miscellaneous	Preliminary Bombardment April 14th And Night April 4/5th 1917	02/04/1917	02/04/1917
Miscellaneous		03/04/1917	03/04/1917
Miscellaneous	Programme Of Firing Day And Night-156th Brigade R.F.A. W Day		
Miscellaneous	Programme Of Firing For X Day And X/Y Night	05/04/1917	05/04/1917
Miscellaneous	Programme Of Firing For "Y" Day	07/04/1917	07/04/1917
Miscellaneous	Lethal And Lachrymatory Shell Bombardment By D/156	05/04/1917	05/04/1917
War Diary	P.C. Ouvrage	05/02/1917	28/02/1917
Miscellaneous	Officer Commanding 156th Brigade R.F.A.	09/02/1917	09/02/1917
Miscellaneous	33rd Division. Summary of Intelligence-28th Feb. 1917	28/02/1917	28/02/1917
War Diary		10/03/1917	12/03/1917
War Diary	Vaux Sur Somme	12/03/1917	31/03/1917
Operation(al) Order(s)	Left Sub Group Order No. 2	31/03/1917	31/03/1917
War Diary	Arras	04/04/1917	12/04/1917
War Diary	Feuchy	13/04/1917	28/04/1917
Miscellaneous	156th Brigade Instruction No. 1	02/04/1917	02/04/1917
Miscellaneous	Amendment No. 1 To Lethal And Lachrymatory Shell Bombardment By D/156 On "Y" Day	06/04/1917	06/04/1917
Miscellaneous	Programme Of Firing "Q" Day And "Q/Y" Night	06/04/1917	06/04/1917
Operation(al) Order(s)	Left Sub-Group Order No. 6	07/04/1917	07/04/1917
Miscellaneous	Barrage Scheme 18 Prs Left Sub-Group	05/04/1917	05/04/1917
Miscellaneous	A Form. Messages And Signals		
Miscellaneous	18prs		
Miscellaneous	Corrections To Left Sub-Group Barrage Scheme	06/04/1917	06/04/1917
Miscellaneous	Barrage Scheme 4.5 Howitzers		
War Diary	(Arras) N Of Feuchy	01/05/1917	03/05/1917
War Diary	Feuchy (Nr Arras)	03/05/1917	31/05/1917
War Diary	In The Field	30/05/1917	30/05/1917
War Diary	Henin	03/06/1917	28/06/1917
War Diary	In The Field Feuchy	05/06/1917	20/06/1917
War Diary	In The Field Henin	21/06/1917	29/06/1917
Miscellaneous	Appendix I 33rd Divisional Artillery	26/06/1917	26/06/1917
Miscellaneous	C.R.A. 3rd Division	19/06/1917	19/06/1917
War Diary		01/07/1917	30/07/1917
War Diary	Coxyde Bains	01/08/1917	01/09/1917
War Diary	Uxem	02/09/1917	02/09/1917
War Diary	Zermezelle	03/09/1917	03/09/1917
War Diary	Renninghelst	04/09/1917	30/09/1917
War Diary	Near Zillebeke	01/10/1917	31/10/1917
War Diary		02/11/1917	23/02/1918
War Diary		21/02/1918	21/02/1918
War Diary	Near Zonnebeke	01/03/1918	30/03/1918
Heading	33rd Divisional Artillery 156th Brigade R.F.A. April 1918		
War Diary	Near Zonnebeke	07/04/1918	30/04/1918
War Diary	Winnezeele	01/05/1918	01/05/1918
War Diary	Nr Brandhoek	08/05/1918	13/05/1918
War Diary	Ch Hord Camp	15/05/1918	30/08/1918
War Diary	Proven Petit Houvain	01/09/1918	01/09/1918
War Diary	Rebreuviette	04/09/1918	16/09/1918
War Diary	Near Heudecourt	16/09/1918	24/09/1918
War Diary	Near Pieziere	29/09/1918	30/09/1918
War Diary	Ossus	01/10/1918	31/10/1918
War Diary	Bertry	01/11/1918	01/11/1918

War Diary	Near Poix	02/11/1918	31/12/1918
War Diary	Brocourt	11/01/1919	01/04/1919
War Diary	Blangy-Sur-Bresle	02/04/1919	28/04/1919
Heading	33 Divisional Artillery 156 Brigade R.F.A. Artillery May 1919 Missing		
War Diary	Blangy S/Bresle	01/06/1919	13/06/1919

WO95/2413 (3)

WO95/2413 (3)

33RD DIVISION
DIVL ARTILLERY

156TH BRIGADE R.F.A.
~~DEC~~ FEB 1915-APR 1919

33

156th Bde: RFA.

Vol: 4

156th Bde: R.F.A.

Vol: I 23

23d

From formation

Dec 15
Apr 19

Instructions regarding War Diaries and Intelligence Summaries are contained in F. S. Regs., Part II. and the Staff Manual respectively. Title Pages will be prepared in manuscript.

WAR DIARY
or
~~INTELLIGENCE~~ SUMMARY
(Erase heading not required.)

(33rd Divl Arty) Sheet 1
156th Bde R.F.A.

Army Form C. 2118

Place	Date	Hour	Summary of Events and Information	Remarks and references to Appendices
GROVE VALE EAST DULWICH LONDON. 3rd Feby 1915.			Summary of Events on the raising of the 33rd Divisional Artillery under War Office letters No 20/Genl No 3670 (A.G.1) dated 14-1-15 and 20/Arty/3838 (A.G.1) dated 3-2-15, addressed to the Mayor of CAMBERWELL, the 156th Brigade R.F.A. commenced recruiting under the Command of Major Fred Hall M.P. — The personnel of this Brigade was complete on 31st March 1915.	
— " —	15.2.15		Captn J F Duncan was appointed Adjutant on 15-2-15. The Brigade was then known as the "CAMBERWELL Gun Brigade"	
— " —	26.3.15		War Office Letter No 20/Arty/3838 (A.G.1.) d/ 26-3-15 authorised the formation of the 162nd Howitzer Brigade — The personnel was complete on 19th April 1915 — Lieut Col. J.F. DUNCAN was given the Command.	
			Authority was then given to complete the Division consisting of 166th, 167th Bgs; 126th Heavy Battery and the 33rd Div Ammn Column	

1875 Wt. W593/826 1,000,000 4/15 J.B.C. & A. A.D.S.S./Forms/C. 2118.

Sheet 2

Army Form C. 2118

Instructions regarding War Diaries and Intelligence Summaries are contained in F. S. Regs., Part II. and the Staff Manual respectively. Title Pages will be prepared in manuscript.

WAR DIARY
or
INTELLIGENCE SUMMARY
(Erase heading not required.)

Place	Date	Hour	Summary of Events and Information	Remarks and references to Appendices
GROVE VALE EAST DULWICH LONDON			Authy was given to designate the 162nd Bge as an 18 pr Bge and the 167th to become the "Howitzer" Brigade – The personnel except for Officers, was complete on 1st Jany 1915, including 1st re-inforcements for the whole Division –	
			Lieut: Col. FRED. HALL was promoted to that rank on 17th April 1915	
			Lieut: Col: J.F. DUNCAN was promoted on 30th April 1915	
—"—	19.3.15		Inspection by Major General Sir T. PERROTT, K.C.B	
—"—	11.4.15		Inspection by Major General Sir FRANCIS LLOYD, KCB. G.O. Comdg London District	
—"—	21.4.15		Inspection by Colonel M. PEAKE, A.A & Q.M.G. Lon. Dist	
—"—	12.5.15		Inspection by Major Genl Sir T. PERROTT K.C.B	
—"—	31.5.15		—do— —do— —do— —do— —do—	
—"—	30.6.15		Divisional Band formed under Bandmaster W. WAY	
—"—	14.7.15		Inspection by Colonel M. PEAKE. C.M.G	
—"—	15.7.15		Equipt, clothing etc taken over by Military Authorities	
—"—	—"—		Inspection by Major General Sir FRANCIS LLOYD. G.O.C. London Dist	

1875 Wt. W593/826 1,000,000 4/15 J.B.C. & A. A.D.S.S./Forms/C. 2118.

Sheet 3

Army Form C. 2118.

Instructions regarding War Diaries and Intelligence Summaries are contained in F. S. Regs., Part II. and the Staff Manual respectively. Title pages will be prepared in manuscript.

WAR DIARY
or
INTELLIGENCE SUMMARY.

(*Erase heading not required.*)

Hour, Date, Place	Summary of Events and Information	Remarks and references to Appendices
GROVE VALE EAST DULWICH LONDON	The Training of the Brigade was carried on in and around DULWICH - Assistance was given at the following centres - Cold Shoeing at HARRODS INSTITUTE, BERMONDSEY, - Artificers were sent to WOOLWICH - men for Cooking were sent to Cooking school - ST. JOHNS WOOD - Map reading by Army School-master WILMOT - FRENCH Classes were held by LADY BATHURST - All officers were sent to either LARK HILL or SHOEBURYNESS on joining.	
	The training Area was too small for a Division - Four 18 pdr Guns were issued in July - Prior to this the Batteries had a Dummy loader each & 3 15/pdr. All Ammtn wagons were issued while at DULWICH - The units were completed with Guns, soon after arrival at BULFORD	

(73989) W4141—463. 400,000. 9/14. H.&J.Ltd. Forms/C. 2118/10.

Sheet 4

Army Form C. 2118.

Instructions regarding War Diaries and Intelligence Summaries are contained in F. S. Regs., Part II. and the Staff Manual respectively. Title pages will be prepared in manuscript.

WAR DIARY
or
INTELLIGENCE SUMMARY.
(*Erase heading not required.*)

Hour, Date, Place	Summary of Events and Information	Remarks and references to Appendices
GROVE VALE EAST DULWICH.	On 9th July 1915, Brigadier Genl W.H. Stuart took Command of the Division	
LONDON. 29.7.15	The 126th Heavy Battery R.G.A. was despatched to NEWCASTLE under the Command of Captain R. C. Aveling. This unit was then Complete in Officers, men & horses.	
	The following arrangements were made as regards Billeting - The 156th Bde & the 33rd Divn Am. Column were billeted at their own homes - The 162nd Bde were at GORDONS Brewery - The 166th Bde at Tramway Depot PECKHAM. This Depot had been converted a Barracks for men, horses & vehicles - The 167th Brigade were at the Baths EAST DULWICH and the 126th Heavy Battery at the Lava Rink DENMARK HILL -	
	All horses were received through the Remount Depot PECKHAM -	
	The Contract for Clothing was given to Messrs Wheeler & Co POULTRY, LONDON	

Sheet 5

Army Form ~~C.~~ 2118.

Instructions regarding War Diaries and Intelligence Summaries are contained in F. S. Regs., Part II. and the Staff Manual respectively. Title pages will be prepared in manuscript.

WAR DIARY
or
INTELLIGENCE SUMMARY.
(Erase heading not required.)

Hour, Date, Place	Summary of Events and Information	Remarks and references to Appendices
	The Divn was moved to BULFORD	
From WATERLOO	on the following dates for training:-	
night 4/5 Aug 15	162nd Brigade to BULFORD in 5 trains	
" 7/8 "	156th " " "	
" 8/9 "	167th " " "	
" 9/10 "	D.A. Col " " "	
" 10/11 "	166th " " "	
	The Division now commenced its training under General W.H. Stuart.	

Sheet 6

Army Form C. 2118.

Instructions regarding War Diaries and Intelligence Summaries are contained in F. S. Regs., Part II. and the Staff Manual respectively. Title pages will be prepared in manuscript.

WAR DIARY
or
INTELLIGENCE SUMMARY. 156th Bgs RFA
(Erase heading not required.)

Hour, Date, Place	Summary of Events and Information	Remarks and references to Appendices
BULFORD 12-8-15	The movement of the Division from LONDON to BULFORD completed - The 156th Bgr took over "D" Lines - The training was carried out under the syllabus laid down in Army Orders	
— " — 25-10-15	Divisional Exercise	
— " — 29-10-15	Divisional Exercise	
" 5-11-15 / do / 9-11-15	Batteries commenced Gun Practice at LARKHILL. Fired 180 Rds each battery. General DRAKE remarked on the good service of the Guns & the drill generally of the detachments	
BULFORD 6-12-15	Received orders for Service overseas - (War Office letter 7.9.QMG	2/609)
— " — 10-12-15	Bgs Amt. Col left AMESBURY for SOUTHAMPTON as follows:-	
— " —	1st Sectn 5-15/m - 2nd Sectn 6-15 pm - 3rd Sectn 7-25 pm	
— " —	Embarked on Transport "MIADAN"	
— " —	Embarkation completed by Amtn Col. at 11-30/pm.	

Sheet 7

Army Form C. 2118.

Instructions regarding War Diaries and Intelligence Summaries are contained in F. S. Regs., Part II. and the Staff Manual respectively. Title pages will be prepared in manuscript.

WAR DIARY
or
INTELLIGENCE SUMMARY.
(Erase heading not required.)

Hour, Date, Place	Summary of Events and Information	Remarks and references to Appendices
SOUTHAMPTON 4.12.15 5 pm	Ammtn: Col: left SOUTHAMPTON arrived HARVE 1-30 AM 12-12-15 Disembarked at 7 am - Rested at GARE MARITIME Point 3 -	Details list of Officers Embarking attached
LE HARVE 13-12-15	Left Point 6 at 11-50 am 13-12-15 - Arrived THIENNES 9-15 am 14-12-15. - Left for MAZINGHEM at 11 am arriving at 2 pm. -	
	The remaining units of Brigade left BULFORD for SOUTHAMPTON on 11th Decr 1915 - Embarking on the Transport "NIRVANA" arriving HARVE on 12th Decr 1915 Disembarked & rested till 13-12-15 - Entrained at GARDE MERCHANDISES commencing at 11-30 am 13-12-15 arriving THIENNES and AIRE on 14-12-15 first train arriving at 7. am - All units marched to billet area MAZINGHEM on 14th Decr 15 last unit arriving 7 - pm	

Sheet 8

Instructions regarding War Diaries and Intelligence Summaries are contained in F. S. Regs., Part II. and the Staff Manual respectively. Title pages will be prepared in manuscript.

WAR DIARY
or
~~INTELLIGENCE~~ SUMMARY.
(Erase heading not required.)

Army Form C. 2118.

156th Bgde RFA

Hour, Date, Place	Summary of Events and Information	Remarks and references to Appendices
MAZINGHEM 15.12.15	The following were the positions of Units at MAZINGHEM	
-"- -"-	Bgde Headquarters. Sheet 36A N.21. a. 9.4	Positions of Headqtrs of Units only.
-"- -"-	A Battery -"- -"- N.17. c 2½.1	
-"- -"-	B -"- -"- -"- N.22. a. 3. 5½	
-"- -"-	C -"- -"- -"- N17 C 3. 1	
-"- -"-	D -"- -"- -"- N17 a 7 2½	
-"- -"-	Bgde Amm Col. -"- -"- N 17. c. 3½. ½	
-"- 18.12.15	Two Officers of A/156 and 16 other Ranks Attached to 15th Battery for Instn	
-"- -"-	Two Officers of C/156 " " " " " " " " " "	
-"- -"-	-"- -"- of B/156 " " " " " 70th " " "	
-"- -"-	" " of D/156 " " " " " 71st " " "	
-"- -"-	One " H.Qrs " " " " " 41st Bgde HQs " "	
-"- 19.12.15	Brigade lined route for farewell of the C-in-C Fieldmarshal Viscount J D P FRENCH. G.C.B. O.M., G.C.V.O. K.C.M.G.	
AIRE 19.12.15	Captn G. Lomer. Special course of lectures by Officers -	
MAZINGHEM 22.12.15	2nd Lieut C.G. BARLOW and 2nd Lieut B. SALL Joined the BDE:	

(73989) W4141—463. 400,000. 9/14. H.&J.Ltd. Forms/C. 2118/10.

Instructions regarding War Diaries and Intelligence Summaries are contained in F. S. Regs., Part II. and the Staff Manual respectively. Title pages will be prepared in manuscript.

WAR DIARY
or
INTELLIGENCE SUMMARY.
(Erase heading not required.)

Sheet 9

Army Form C. 2118.

Hour, Date, Place		Summary of Events and Information	Remarks and references to Appendices
MAZINGHEM	22.12.15	Parties attached to Batteries 2nd Divl Arty returned	
—"—	—"—	Two Officer & 16 other ranks A/156 attached to 15th	Battery 2nd Divn
—"—	—"—	—"— —"— —"— —"— B/156 —"— "70th	—"— —"—
—"—	—"—	—"— —"— —"— —"— C/156 —"— "40th	—"— —"—
—"—	—"—	—"— —"— —"— —"— D/156 —"— "17th	—"— ——
—"—	—"—	—— 4 —"— —"— HQrs —"— "41st Bge	—"—
—"—	26-12-15	The above parties returned to MAZINGHEM	
—"—	26.12.15	Right Sectn A/156 with Sectn Comdr attached to 15th	Battery
—"—	—"—	—"— —"— B/156 —"— —"— —"— —"— to 70th	—"—
—"—	—"—	Colonel F HALL attached to 41st Bde R.F.A.	
—"—	—"—	One Officer 2 NCOs & 1 Servant attached to 34th	Bge Am Col
—"—	—"—	Major H ALLCARD attached to 15th Battery. 2nd Divn	
—"—	30.12.15	Above parties returned to MAZINGHEM	
—"—	30.12.15	Right Sectn C/156 with Sectn Comdr attached to 15th	Battery
—"—	—"—	—"— —"— D/156 —"— —"— —"— —"— "71st	—"—
—"—	—"—	One Officer 2 NCOs & 1 Servant attached to 34th	Bge Am Col

(73989) W4141—463. 400,000. 9/14. H.&J.Ltd. Forms/C. 2118/10.

Sheet 10

Army Form C. 2118.

Instructions regarding War Diaries and Intelligence Summaries are contained in F. S. Regs., Part II. and the Staff Manual respectively. Title pages will be prepared in manuscript.

WAR DIARY
or
INTELLIGENCE SUMMARY.
(*Erase heading not required.*)

156th Bde R.F.A. Jany 1916

Hour, Date, Place		Summary of Events and Information	Remarks and references to Appendices
MAZINGHEM	4-1-16	Left Sectn A/156 with Sectn Comdrs attached to 15th Battery 2nd Divn	
— " —	— " —	" " B/156 — " — " — " 70th — " — "	
— " —	5-1-16 9.15 am	Batty Officers & Amn Column Tactical Exercises under Bde Major	
— " —	— " —	Right Sect "C" & "D" return from firing line -	
— " —	6-1-16	Gas Demonstration for Bde by 1st Army Gas Expert	
— " —	7-1-16	Left Sectn "A" & "B" return from firing line.	
— " —	— " —	Col F Hall left for England to take part in debate in House of Commons	
— " —	11-1-16	Major H Allcard & 3 officers with 4 Gun Battery Detachments	
	— " —	took over A/64 Bde 12th Divn: in firing line.	
	— " —	Captn R.D. Russell & 2 officers with Capt Talbot of "D" Battery	
	— " —	took over B/64 Bde: 12th Divn in firing line.	
— " —	14-1-16	Col F. Hall returned from England -	
— " —	18-1-16	"A" & "B" Batteries return from firing line -	
— " —	19-1-16	Major H. Allcard posted to 32nd Divn: as Bde Comdr	
— " —	19-1-16	Captn L.R. Hill posted Bde (Vice Allcard) from 6th Divn and to Comd "A"/156 Bde:	

Sheet 11

Army Form C. 2118.

Instructions regarding War Diaries and Intelligence Summaries are contained in F. S. Regs., Part II. and the Staff Manual respectively. Title pages will be prepared in manuscript.

WAR DIARY
or
INTELLIGENCE SUMMARY.

(*Erase heading not required.*)

156th Bde RFA. Jany 16

Hour, Date, Place	Summary of Events and Information	Remarks and references to Appendices
MAZINGHEM 20.1.16	Brigade finé route for General Joffre C. in C Allied Forces in France	
—"— 26.1.16	Brigade parade for Inspn. by Genl Gough Corps Comdr.	
—"— 30.1.16	Divisional Tactical Exercise to THEROUANNE	
31.1.16	—"— —"— —"— completed & returned to Billets.	
	During the month Horse standings had been advanced	
	The A.D.V.S reported on them "as being the best in the 1st Army when completed" Also satisfactory reports on horses.	
	The A.D.M.S gave good report on condition of Billets.	
	Batteries exercised in all methods of Drill.	
	Helio was used on very clear moonlight nights - Lamps were also used. Gun Drill & Alarms practised at all times day & night. Map reading was tested by Brigade Major. Telephonists were attached to Signals periodically for instruction & refreshers.	
" 15.2.16	Major H Rochfort-Boyd DSO RFA assumed command vice Lt Col Fred Hall who returned to England	
17.2.16	W G Pringle 2nd Lt RFA appointed acting adjutant vice W Holden Lieut. RFA who accompanied Lt Col Hall	

Officers with B.E.F. on departure for Service Overseas.

156th BRIGADE, R.F.A. 33rd DIVISION.

	Lieutenant-Colonel	Hall, F.
Adj.	Lieutenant	Holden, W. (R)
O.O.	2nd Lieutenant	Oxley, B.L. (T.C.)

MAJORS.

A. Allcard, H. (R.)
B.
C.
D.

CAPTAINS.

A.
B. Russell, R.D. (T.C.)
C. Lomer, G. (T.C.)
D. Talbot, S. (R.)
A.C. Campbell, J. (R.)

SUBALTERNS.

A.(2) Pringle, W.G. (T.C.)
(2) Challen, J.D. (T.C.)
(2) Stuart, D. (T.C.)

B.(2) Prior, L.M.S. (T.C.)
(2) Baldwin, H.D. (T.C.)
(2) Tayler, H. (T.C.)

C.(2) Vick, D.B. (T.C.)
(2) Prior, E.H. (T.C.)
(2) Vestey, L. (T.C.)

D.(2) Turner, K.F.S. (T.C.)
(2) Bloor, C.A. (T.C.)
(2) Sheeres, W.G. (T.C.)

A.C.(2) Mitchell, A. (T.C.)
(2) Elliott, M.A. (T.C.)
(2) Wingate, T. (T.C.)

Lieutenant. Eady, L.F. (A.V.C.) (T.C.)

Lieutenant Campbell, J. (R.A.M.C.) (T.C.)

Confidential

War Diary

of

156th Bde RFA

from Feb 1st 1916 to March 1st 1916

Sheet I

Instructions regarding War Diaries and Intelligence Summaries are contained in F. S. Regs., Part II. and the Staff Manual respectively. Title pages will be prepared in manuscript.

WAR DIARY
or
~~INTELLIGENCE SUMMARY~~.
(Erase heading not required.)

Army Form C. 2118.

156th Bde RFA

Hour, Date, Place			Summary of Events and Information	Remarks and references to Appendices
		~~4.2.16~~	~~Capt L R Hill assumed command during absence of Lt Col F. Hall~~	
MAZINGHEM		5.2.16	1 A/Bomdr + 6 men were exchanged by each Bty with Am. Col so that the Column men could receive instruction in gun drill etc.	
"	8 am.	6.2.16	Divine service in School House	
		7.2.16	2Lt A Mitchell proceeded for attachment to 2nd Div. Arty for instructional purposes.	
		" " "	Three Signallers sent on Course at BERGUETTE	
		" " "	5 NCOs from 2nd Div Arty posted to Am Col, and 2 to 'A' Bty & 1 to 'C' Bty, under recommendation for Promotion	
	2.30 pm	8.2.16	The ADVS inspected the horses of the Brigade reporting favourably.	
	11 pm	9.2.16	2Lt J.D Challen 'A' Bty & 2 Sgts conveyed to 1st Army Artillery School LIETTRES	
	2 pm	9.2.16	Inspection of Billet Stores by Lt Col F. Hall	
		9.2.16	Lt Col F Hall having been absent on special leave in England since 4th Feb, returned. Capt L.R Hill relinquishes temporary command.	

WP.

Sheet 2

Instructions regarding War Diaries and Intelligence Summaries are contained in F. S. Regs., Part II. and the Staff Manual respectively. Title pages will be prepared in manuscript.

WAR DIARY
or
~~INTELLIGENCE~~ SUMMARY.
(*Erase heading not required.*)

Army Form C. 2118.

Hour, Date, Place		Summary of Events and Information	Remarks and references to Appendices
MAZINGHEM	10.2.16	No 6060 Sgt Edwards C.H. 'A' Bty left for England on promotion to 2nd Lieut —	
" 9.30am	13.2.16	1 signaller from each Bty & HQ Staff proceeded to H.Q. 167th Bde RFA to attend a course of Telephony at BERGUETTE	
"	15.2.16	Half the Brigade proceeded to AIRE for Baths — Change of underclothing being issued	
"	16.2.16	The Remainder of the Brigade proceeded to AIRE for Baths —	
" 6 pm	16.2.16	H Rochfort-Boyd DSO RFA joined the Brigade & assumed command	
9 pm.	16.2.16	Lt Col Fred Hall RFA & W Holden Lt & adjutant departed for England	
9 pm	16.2.16	W.G. Pringle 2Lt R.F.A. assumed the duty of adjutant	

WGP

(73989) W4141—463. 400,000. 9/14. H.&J.Ltd. Forms/C. 2118/10.

Feb 1916

Sheet 3

Army Form C. 2118.

WAR DIARY
or
~~INTELLIGENCE SUMMARY~~. 156th Bde RFA Feby 1916

(Erase heading not required.)

Instructions regarding War Diaries and Intelligence Summaries are contained in F. S. Regs., Part II. and the Staff Manual respectively. Title pages will be prepared in manuscript.

Hour, Date, Place		Summary of Events and Information	Remarks and references to Appendices
MAZINGHEM	17-2-16	2Lt T Wingate proceeded to STVENANT for attachment to a Trench Mortar Bty, having volunteered for this duty	
"		2Lt B Sall transferred from 'D' Bty to Am. Col & absorbed	
"	19.2.16	2Lt HFS Turner proceeded to 12th Div Arty. for attachment for the purpose of being instructed in position to be taken over by 'D' Bty at a later date	
"	19.2.16	A number of NCOs transferred from the 2nd Div Arty to this unit, under recommendation for promotion, were duly promoted & posted to Batteries and Am. Cl.	
"	21.2.16	Paint and Turpentine having been issued, Painting of Divisional Marks on vehicles was proceeded with	
"	22.2.16	The Signalling Classes at BERGUETTE & CHOCQUES being dismissed the NCOs & men returned to MAZINGHEM and ROMBLY	

WB

(73989) W4141—463. 400,000. 9/14. H.&J.Ltd. Forms/C. 2118/10.

Sheet 4

Instructions regarding War Diaries and Intelligence Summaries are contained in F. S. Regs., Part II. and the Staff Manual respectively. Title pages will be prepared in manuscript.

WAR DIARY
or
~~INTELLIGENCE SUMMARY~~.
(Erase heading not required.)

Army Form C. 2118.

156th Bde RFA

Hour, Date, Place	Summary of Events and Information	Remarks and references to Appendices
MAZINGHEM (21).2.16	Major H Rochfort-Boyd DSO RFA, Capt L R Hill RFA Capt R D Russell RFA proceeded to the line with a view to reconnoitring positions to be taken over on following day. The senior officer left in Billets was Capt. S Talbot RFA	
23.2.16	5 Signallers of H Q Staff proceeded to 12th Div. Arty O.P. exchange	
10 am " "	4 Signallers one each from A, B, D, Bty and Amm Col conveyed by motor Lorry to school of Instruction at BETHUNE	
5 45 am	One section of A, D, B Batteries and wagon line party of C Bty proceeded to take over positions hitherto occupied by 64th Bde RFA at QUINCHY. The Guns, with sights stores & spare parts were left behind & handed over with list of Deficiencies & means of examination to the incoming sections of 64th Bde — The Gun detachments were conveyed by MOTOR ~~Lorry~~ BUS to the line, baggage being conveyed by 2 Lorries — The Roads were slippery, but Frost Cogs had been fitted	

Army Form C. 2118.

Instructions regarding War Diaries and Intelligence Summaries are contained in F. S. Regs., Part II. and the Staff Manual respectively. Title pages will be prepared in manuscript.

WAR DIARY
or
~~INTELLIGENCE SUMMARY~~.
(Erase heading not required.)

156th Bde RFA

Hour, Date, Place		Summary of Events and Information	Remarks and references to Appendices
MAZINGHEM cont.	23.2.16	fitted & no casualties occurred – 200 Rds of Shrapnel were handed over to incoming sections of 64th Bde –	
	24.2.16	Capt L R Hill having returned from the line assumed Command vice Capt S Talbot	
5.30 am.	25.2.16	The Remaining Sections marched out of MAZINGHEM & ROMBLY taking their two guns & complement of ammunition – The Guns & 150 Rds Shrapnel & 50 Rds H E were handed over to 64th Bde at wagon lines BETHUNE (see map coordinates sheet 8)	
9 am	25.2.16	Motor Busses conveyed the Detachments to Gun Positions (see map coordinates sheet 8) Lorries conveying any baggage that could not be taken in wagons, baggage as far as it was possible one officer went with wagon line party and one with [struck out], gun detachments of each section –	
	25.2.16	W G Pringle 2nd Lt a/adj was appointed Adjutant with effect from 17.2.16	WGP

463. 400,000. 9/14. H.&J.Ltd. Forms/C. 2118/10.

Sheet 6

Army Form C. 2118.

Instructions regarding War Diaries and Intelligence Summaries are contained in F. S. Regs., Part II. and the Staff Manual respectively. Title pages will be prepared in manuscript.

WAR DIARY
or
INTELLIGENCE SUMMARY.

(Erase heading not required.)

156th Bde RFA

Hour, Date, Place	Summary of Events and Information	Remarks and references to Appendices
MAZINGHEM 5.30 a.m. 26.2.16	The Amn Column marched out of Billets & proceeded via LILLERS, CHOCQUES, to where it stayed one night, moving next morning to BETHUNE	
27.2.16	(See map Coordinate, Sheet 8)	
" 9 a.m. 27.2.16	The HQ Staff marched out of ROMBLY proceeding via LILLERS CHOCQUES VENDIN-LES-BETHUNE to BETHUNE; the horses were stabled in a disused distillery, the 3 vehicles being parked outside. The Brigade office was established at 9 Rue Gambetta — The men were billeted in the Barracks —	
BETHUNE		
" 8.30 a.m. 28.2.16	Supplies for the Brigade drawn by units from Marché Chevaux BETHUNE.	
11 a.m.	Post collected from the Quay, Canal —	
27.2.16	2nd Lt / D Challen completed the course at LIETTRES and returned to duty with 'A' Bty	WP

(73989) W4141—463. 400,000. 9/14. H.&J.Ltd. Forms/C. 2118/10.

Sheet 7

Army Form C. 2118.

Instructions regarding War Diaries and Intelligence Summaries are contained in F. S. Regs., Part II. and the Staff Manual respectively. Title pages will be prepared in manuscript.

WAR DIARY
or
~~INTELLIGENCE SUMMARY~~.

(*Erase heading not required.*)

Hour, Date, Place	Summary of Events and Information	Remarks and references to Appendices
BETHUNE 28.2.16	2Lt M A Elliott RFA transferred from 'C' Bty to D Bty for duty, during the absence of	
6 pm " "	2Lt W.G. Sheares RFA reported at 1st army artillery school LIETTRES.	
29.2.16	A bootmaker was established in Am. Col. Saddlers shops to attend to repairs of boots belonging to men in the Bde.	
GENERAL.	During the first 20 days of the month Horse Standings were greatly advanced & ~~covered~~ overhead cover erected. Billets were satisfactory & a certificate was obtained from the MO. stating that they were left clean & in a hygienic condition on vacation. Batteries were exercised daily in all methods of drill, particular attention being paid to Mounted Drill & Tactics with a definite scheme prepared beforehand. Signalling in all branches was carried on	WGP

Sheet 8

Army Form C. 2118.

Instructions regarding War Diaries and Intelligence Summaries are contained in F. S. Regs., Part II. and the Staff Manual respectively. Title pages will be prepared in manuscript.

WAR DIARY
or
~~INTELLIGENCE~~ SUMMARY.

(Erase heading not required.)

156th Bde RFA

Hour, Date, Place	Summary of Events and Information		Remarks and references to Appendices
BETHUNE Feb 23rd to Feb 29th	Gun Positions as taken over from 64th Bde		
	A 6th Ed. of Sheet 36 (Combined)	A 13 b 2.4.	
	B + ½ D " "	F 18 a 3.0.	
	C " "	F 24 c 6.2.	
	½ D " "	A 14 d 3.7.	
	Wagon Lines as now occupied		
	A 6th Ed. of Sheet 36 BETHUNE combined	F 7 a 5.8.	
	B " "	F 9 a 1.3.	
	C " "	E 12 a 4.9.	
	D " "	F 7 a 5.8	
	Am Col " "	E 5 c 8.8	

156 RFA
Vol 5

CONFIDENTIAL

WAR DIARY
of

156th Bde RFA

from March 1st 1916 to March 31st. 1916

Volume 5

Sheet 3.

Army Form C. 2118.

Instructions regarding War Diaries and Intelligence Summaries are contained in F. S. Regs., Part II. and the Staff Manual respectively. Title pages will be prepared in manuscript.

WAR DIARY
or
~~INTELLIGENCE~~ SUMMARY.
(*Erase heading not required.*)

156th Bde RFA

Hour, Date, Place	Summary of Events and Information	Remarks and references to Appendices
ANNEQUIN March 1st 1916	The batteries remained in action as follows (sheet 36, combined BETHUNE) A/156 – A 13 B 4 – 6 – (attached 38th Div) B/156 F 18 A 4½ 2 (also ½ B/156) C/156 F 24 C 7 . 4 ½ D/156 A 14 D 4 . 7 (attached AUCHY GROUP) The attachments of A. 156 + a section of D/156 being for tactical purposes only – The Brigade office which was incorporated in A Group (later QUINCHY GROUP) was at F 23 B 3,8. The Zone covered by A/156 was from A 16 C 5 5½ (the North Bank of LA BASSEE CANAL, where crossed by the German front line trench) to A 16 A 2½ 7½ (Point 37). This allotment lies in the area of the 38th Divn ZONE covered by B/156 and a section of D/156 from A 16 C 5 5½ to A 22 A 3 6	

WP

Sheet 4.

Army Form C. 2118.

Instructions regarding War Diaries and Intelligence Summaries are contained in F. S. Regs., Part II. and the Staff Manual respectively. Title pages will be prepared in manuscript.

WAR DIARY
or
INTELLIGENCE SUMMARY.
(Erase heading not required.)

152' Bde RFA

Hour, Date, Place	Summary of Events and Information	Remarks and references to Appendices
ANNEQUIN N March 1st	ZONE covered [illegible] C/156 A22A 36 to A22A 2 4½ a section of D/156 [illegible] QUINCHY STATION [illegible] Z (AUCHY GROUP) [illegible] purposes – No casualties were inflicted by the enemy during the month and no damage was done to material other than of an insignificant nature except to No 1 gun [illegible] action of A/156 which was damaged by a stray 5.9 on March 11th – This gun was [illegible] exchanged for a new one. During the month, a great deal of work was carried out many additions + reinforcements to emplacements being made. O.P.s were improved + the telephone system reorganised – At the wagon lines work was continually in progress improving standings + clearing the lines – A number of NCOs + men were sent on courses of Artillery instruction, signalling, Telephony	

[illegible]

(73989) W4141—463. 400,000. 9/14. H.&J.Ltd. Forms/C. 2118/10.

Sheet 5.

Instructions regarding War Diaries and Intelligence Summaries are contained in F. S. Regs., Part II. and the Staff Manual respectively. Title pages will be prepared in manuscript.

WAR DIARY
or
~~INTELLIGENCE~~ SUMMARY.
(*Erase heading not required.*)

156 Bde RFA

Army Form C. 2118.

Hour, Date, Place	Summary of Events and Information	Remarks and references to Appendices
ANNEQUIN N March	telephony and cooking and in general the standard showed appreciable improvement – The wagon line of D/156 after being moved from F7A58 to E6C46 was again transferred to E5D38., the first billet being too crowded & the second being required for a battalion of infantry —. Hostile shelling during this month was not directed against any battery position, but the OPs were occasionally shelled without suffering material damage – Aeroplane scouts were posted during daylight & on the approach of a hostile plane a whistle was blown & all movement in the vicinity was stopped Lamp signalling was employed from the trenches & tested every evening, as a precaution against failure of telephone communication. The condition of the horses suffered somewhat owing to climatic conditions & lack of regular exercise in draft, and one death has to be recorded	HRP H. Rochfort Boyd Lt Col Cmdg 156th Bde RFA

(73989) W4141—463. 400,000. 9/14. H.&J.Ltd. Forms/C. 2118/10.

Sheet 1

Army Form C. 2118.

Instructions regarding War Diaries and Intelligence Summaries are contained in F. S. Regs., Part II. and the Staff Manual respectively. Title pages will be prepared in manuscript.

WAR DIARY
or
INTELLIGENCE SUMMARY.
(Erase heading not required.)

156th Bde RFA

Hour, Date, Place	Summary of Events and Information	Remarks and references to Appendices
ANNEQUIN N		
6-3-16	LIGHT GOOD and a lot of Registration was carried out.	
	Night firing at working parties at intervals during the night.	
11.3.16 2 pm	B/156 carried out wire cutting at A 16 c 7.4.	
13-3-16	B/156 carried out wire cutting at A 15 c 7½ 4 in co-operation with B/162 – and during the night Howitzer fire was directed against the Trenches at this point to prevent repair of the damage done	
15.3.16 16.3.16	B/156 continued wire cutting & a narrow lane was effected right through the enemy's wire.	
17.3.16	B/156 continued wire cutting but the wind proved too gusty for accurate shooting	
	2Lt FW Beadle posted to A Bty	
	2Lt CF Woodroffe — B —	
	2Lt LH White — C	
18.3.16	7485 BSM Davison RB posted to Am Col vice BSM Monahan commissioned	
	45047 BSM Wilcock D posted to B Bty vice BSM Jenkins transferred –	
19.3.16	47427 Sgt FG Cowey posted to 162nd Bde on promotion	KP.

Sheet 2

Instructions regarding War Diaries and Intelligence Summaries are contained in F. S. Regs., Part II. and the Staff Manual respectively. Title pages will be prepared in manuscript.

WAR DIARY
or
INTELLIGENCE SUMMARY.
(*Erase heading not required.*)

Army Form C. 2118.

156 Bde RFA

Hour, Date, Place	Summary of Events and Information	Remarks and references to Appendices
ANNEQUIN N 19.3.16 10 am	Inspection of AVC sergeants at 43rd MVS BETHUNE	
22.3.16	2Lt M.A. Elliott proceeded to LIETTRES on a course of instruction at 1st Army Artillery School	
28.3.16	BQMS Spank in B/156 posted to 162 Bde on promotion	
29.3.16 7.40 pm	~~A~~ a section of C/156 proceeded to Vermelles G7B81 for enfilade Purposes.	
30.3.16	Registration of Brickstacks ABC was carried out	
"	BQMS Peacock (No 60730) posted to B/156	
31-3-16	2Lt PK Margoris posted to Bde & attached to C Bty	

AP

156 RFA
Vol ~~3~~6

XXXIII

CONFIDENTIAL

War Diary
of
156th F.A. Bde

from April 1st. to April 30th

Volume

2nd Sheet

Army Form C. 2118.

WAR DIARY
or
~~INTELLIGENCE~~ SUMMARY. 156th F A BDE

(Erase heading not required.)

Instructions regarding War Diaries and Intelligence Summaries are contained in F. S. Regs., Part II. and the Staff Manual respectively. Title pages will be prepared in manuscript.

Hour, Date, Place	Summary of Events and Information	Remarks and references to Appendices
ANNEQUIN N 1 – 4 – 16 2 pm to 3 am	B/156 ½ D/156 & C/156 cooperated with the GROUP in preparing the ground for a raid made by the 98th INF BDE & making a barrage while the infantry were out – The OC. Group also controlled the Trench Mortar battery which did good work –	Appendix I WJP Appendix II
2 – 4 – 16	2nd Lt H TAYLER proceeded on leave to ENGLAND for 7 days	WJP
7 – 4 – 16	2nd Lt H D BALDWIN proceeded to a course of instruction with 18th Anti Aircraft Battery –	WJP
15 – 4 – 16	A/156 proceeded to F7A 7.7 (then wagon lines) and remained there during the remainder of the month –	WJP
16 – 4 – 16	2nd Lt M S PRIOR attended a Course of Horse Management for two hours daily for 15 working days —	WJP
17. 4 – 16	2nd Lt D B ~~VICK~~ promoted to LIEUT was transferred to B.A.C. 2nd Lt B SALL transferred from BAC to A Bty.	WJP
22. 4. 16 24 4 16 25. 4. 16 10 pm 10.40 pm	Veterinary Inspection by D.D.S. 2nd Lt M A ELLIOTT proceeded to ST VENANT on Trench Mortar Course Artillery preparation in conjunction with Infantry Raid on CRATERS S of LA BASSEE Road –	WJP WJP Appendix II
30 – 4 – 16	2nd Lt J.D. CHALLEN proceeded to BOULOGNE on course of instruction with I Bty RHA —	WJP

(73989) W4141—463. 400,000. 9/14. H.&J.Ltd. Forms/C. 2118/10.

Instructions regarding War Diaries and Intelligence Summaries are contained in F. S. Regs., Part II. and the Staff Manual respectively. Title pages will be prepared in manuscript.

WAR DIARY
or
~~INTELLIGENCE SUMMARY~~.
(Erase heading not required.)

Army Form C. 2118.

156TH F.A. BDE

1st Sheet

Hour, Date, Place	Summary of Events and Information	Remarks and references to Appendices
ANNEQUIN N. April 1st – 30th 1916	The Brigade remained in action incorporated in the CUINCHY GROUP as regards B/156, C/156 & ½ D/156 – A/156 up to the 15th was attached to B GROUP N of the CANAL (AIRE à LA BASSEE –) ½ D/156 was attached to AUCHY GROUP for tactical purposes. Lt Col H. Rochfort-Boyd DSO RFA was the GROUP commander as during March Lt W. G. Pringle RFA — — Adjutant — — 2Lt B. L. Otley RFA —— Orderly officer — — During the month progress was made in relaying & strengthening the telephone system – rebuilding gun pits & dug-outs – The condition of the horses showed great improvement all round and was favourable commented on by the D.D.S. Every opportunity was taken of sending officers and other ranks on Gunnery and other courses –	HRB H. Rochfort-Boyd Cr 156th Bde

(73989) W4141—463. 400,000. 9/14. H.&J.Ltd. Forms/C. 2118/10.

WAR DIARY
Appendix I

Detail of Artillery Employed

No.		Time	Ammunition	Target	Fired from.
Mortars					
4	2" Mortars	0 mins to 5 mins 5 mins to 7 mins 7 mins to 20 mins	30 HE 8 Smoke Shells 70 HE	Crater X Placed according to the wind Trenches W. of A.B. & C. Brickstacks	Close to No 9 BRICKSTACK
2	1½" Mortars	0 mins to 5 mins 5 mins to 20 mins	15 HE 35 HE	Crater X Trenches W of A B & C BRICKSTACKS	Close to No 9 BRICKSTACK
5	3½" Light Mortars	30 Secs to 20 mins	100 HE	Trenches A 22 a 22 to 24	Trenches S of No 1 BRICKSTACK
2	Stokes	30 Secs to 5 mins 5 mins to 20 mins	50 HE 150 HE	Crater Y Trenches between CRATER Y & "A" BRICKSTACK	Close in front of No 9 BRICKSTACK
Howitzers					
2	4.5 Hows.	30 Secs to 20 mins	120 HE	BRICKSTACKS N. of "D" BRICKSTACK	
4	6 Hows.	1 min to 20 mins	22 HE	Neighbourhood of A.22 b.2.5	
18 Pounders					
2	C/156	30 Secs to 20 mins	120 Shrapnel	A.B. & C BRICKSTACKS	VERMELLES
2	B/162	30 secs to 20 mins	40 HE & Shrap	Trenches A 22 a 22 to 2.4.	TOURBIERES
2	B/156	30 Secs to 20 mins	40 HE & Shrap.	Trenches near "H" BRICKSTACK	Canal

TELEPHONIC COMMUNICATION

Central Direction	Lt. Col Rochfort-Boyd	No 9 BRICKSTACK	
Liaison officer	Capt Havell	Crater D Metallic Circuit No. 9	Brickstack to Crater B
O's. C. B/162 and	C/156	MOUNTAIN HOUSE Metallic Circuit No. 9	Brickstack to MOUNTAIN HOUSE
FOO A/167 and	O.C B/156	KINGSCLERE Metallic Circuit No. 9	Brickstack to KINGSCLERE

[illegible]

B.M.O/158 3rd.

WAR DIARY
Appendix II

Lieut-Col. H. Rochfort-Boyd, D.S.O.

In forwarding the attached for your information, I wish to emphasise my very keen appreciation of the arrangements made by you and the manner in which they were carried out by those under your command. It was due to the very co[m]plete and thorough preparation of the ground by the Artillery and T.Ms that the Infantry were enabled to carry out their part as they did.

(SD) E.P.Strickland, Brig-General,
Commanding 98th Brigade.

Certified true copy

[illegible signature] Lt & Adj
156th Bde RFA

War Diary Appendix III

No.		Time.	Ammn.	Target.
4.	2" Mortars	0 mins to 12 mins 12 mins to 15 mins 15 mins to 60 mins	32 H.E. 8 smoke 80 H.E.	N & S Gaps. Barrage (Res. Line) Barrage (Res. Line)
4.	Stokes Mortars	0 mins to 12 mins 12 mins to 6D mins	60 H.E. 140 H.E.	Area of Raid. Barrage (Res. Line)
2.	3.7"Mortars	0 mins to 60 mins	100 H.E.	A.B.C.Brickstacks.
2.	6" Hows.	0 mins to 6 mins 6 mins to 12 mins 12 mins to 60 mins	12 H.E. 12 H.E. 16 H.E.	N & S Gaps. Support Line. A.Brickstack & Frank's Keep.
3.	4.5" Hows.	0 mins to 60 mins	80 H.E.	Frank's Keep (Res. Line) Brickstacks.
D/166	4-18 prs.	0 mins to 60 mins	50 H.E. & Shrap.	Front & Sòpport Trenches.
C/162	4-18 prs.	0 mins to 60 mins	100 H.E. & Shrap.	Front and Support Trenches.
B/162	3-18 prs.	0 mins to 6 mins 6 mins to 60 mins	30 Shrap 70 H.E. & Shrap.	Area of Raid Barrage (Res. Line)
C/156	4-18 prs.	0 mins to 60 mins	100 H.E. & Shrap.	Front & Support Trenches & Brickstacks.
B/156	2-18 prs.	0 mins to 60 mins	50 H.E. & Shrap.	Embankment and Brickstacks.

The Raid is timed for O 15 mins. Central direction from White House.
Watches will be synchronized and all times will be by watch.

[illegible signature] 23 [illegible]

156 RFA

Vol 4

Confidential

War Diary

of

33

156th Bde RFA

from May 1st 1916 to May 31st 1916

Volume

Sheet I

Army Form C. 2118.

Instructions regarding War Diaries and Intelligence Summaries are contained in F. S. Regs., Part II. and the Staff Manual respectively. Title pages will be prepared in manuscript.

WAR DIARY or ~~INTELLIGENCE SUMMARY.~~

(Erase heading not required.)

156th BDE RFA

Place	Date	Hour	Summary of Events and Information	Remarks and references to Appendices
	MAY			
ANNEQUIN	2nd		2Lt M.A. ELLIOTT RFA returned to duty having complete a course of instruction in TRENCH MORTARS at St VENANT	WP
	12th		2Lt J.D. CHALLEN RFA " " " " " " " " " " " ARTILLERY WORK at BOULOGNE with I Troop RFA	WP
	19th		The BAC under command of CAPT J.S. CAMPBELL RFA becomes absorbed into the 33 DAC the majority of men & horses forming No1 Section A Echelon –	
			D/156 under command of CAPT S. TALBOT RFA becomes A/167	
			A/167 Howitzer " " " CAPT M.A. STUDD RFA " D/156	WP
	23rd	4pm	Bombardment of enemy's trenches 120 yards south of LA BASSEE ROAD	Appendix I
	23rd	10.30pm		I^A
	24th	12.15am		I^B
	24th	2.30am		I^C
	25th		28427 BSM GLOSSOP C A/156 departed for the purpose of taking up a commission	
	27th		Lt COL H ROCHFORT-BOYD RFA proceeded to England on leave the command of the Bde devolved upon CAPT L.R. HILL RFA	WP
	27th		The headquarters office was moved from ANNEQUIN N. to 31 Rue GAMBETTA BETHUNE	

T2134. Wt. W708–776. 500000. 4/15. Sir J. C. & S.

2nd Sheet

Army Form C. 2118.

Instructions regarding War Diaries and Intelligence Summaries are contained in F. S. Regs., Part II. and the Staff Manual respectively. Title pages will be prepared in manuscript.

WAR DIARY
or
INTELLIGENCE SUMMARY.
(Erase heading not required.)

156th BDE RFA

Place	Date	Hour	Summary of Events and Information	Remarks and references to Appendices
	MAY			
ANNEQUIN	27th		Capt L R HILL RFA being wounded in action, the command was assumed by Capt M A STUDD RFA.	WSP
	28th		Lt E G LUTYENS RFA Adjutant 166th Bde RFA posted to command (temporarily) A/156 —	WSP

T2134. Wt. W708–776. 500000. 4/15. Sir J. C. & S.

3rd Sheet

Army Form C. 2118.

Instructions regarding War Diaries and Intelligence Summaries are contained in F. S. Regs., Part II. and the Staff Manual respectively. Title pages will be prepared in manuscript.

WAR DIARY
or
~~INTELLIGENCE SUMMARY.~~
(Erase heading not required.)

156th Bde RFA

Place	Date	Hour	Summary of Events and Information	Remarks and references to Appendices
	MAY			
ANNEQUIN	1st to 31st		The brigade Remained in action, incorporated in CUINCHY GROUP, with B/162 C/162, D/166 + (till the reorganisation of the Brigade) A 167 + ½ C 167 Howitzers —	
			During this month the Group was under the command of Lt Col H ROCHFORT-BOYD DSO RFA; the Adjutant was Lt W. G. PRINGLE RFA; the orderly officer 2Lt B L OXLEY RFA — until the 27th of the month when the headquarters staff of the 167th Bde relieved —	
			A/156 returned from the training area + went into the line at G 2 A 5.6. as counter battery, from 3rd of May to the end of the month —	
			The gun positions were in some cases rebuilt + strengthened, steel cupolas being used, the telephonic communications were extended + improved —	
			At the wagon lines, the condition + appearance of the horses was reported upon by the D.D.V.S. as being very satisfactory —	
			Four officers + 26 men proceeded on 7 days leave to England.	WP
				HRB Lt Col

Copy A 4

Appendix I

It is proposed to carry out an operation against the German front line system of Trenches 120 yards South of the LA BASSEE Road.

At this spot the German front trench is in full view of and under fire from our trenches.

The operation will be in two phases.

1st Phase at 4 p.m.

The destruction of his front line trenches so as to make a gap which he will try to repair at night, while at the same time he will fear a raid.

2nd Phase at 10.30 p.m., 12.15 a.m. and 2.30 a.m.

To keep the damage unrepaired and to cause loss to the enemy manning the damaged parapets.

Three five minute bombardments of his front line trench. After five minutes the range will be lengthened as if for a raid, i.e. from 5 mins till 10 mins.

After allowing two minutes for the enemy to come out and man his parapet, the Enfilade section will commence and will sweep the line at a rapid rate of fire from 7 mins till 10 minutes.

Total expenditure of ammunition :-

	1st Phase.	2nd Phase.	Total.
2" Mortars	150	120	270
Stokes Mortars	nil	180	180
9.2" Hows	30 H.E.	nil	30
6" Hows	4 H.E.	36	40
4.5" Hows	10 H.E.	150	160
18 - prs	100 H.E. & Shrapnel	600	700

I A

PROGRAMME OF 1st PHASE. ZERO TIME 4 p.m.

No.		Time.	Ammn.	Target.
11	2" Mortars	0 mins to about 60 mins	150 H.E.	A circle closing in gradually to the same spot in front line trench
1	9.2 How.	0 mins till finished	30 H.E.	Starting over the Target ~~[illegible]~~? gradually coming down to it, then keeping on same spot so as to thoroughly destroy the trenches in one limited locality.
2	6" Hows	After the 9.2 has finished	4 H.E.	Registration for the night. Start as soon as the 9.2 has finished
3	4.5 Hows.	After the 6" has finished.	10 H.E.	Registration for the night. Start as soon as the 6" has finished.
8	18 - prs.	0 mins to about 60 mins	100 H.E. delay & Shrapnel	A circle to catch the troops withdrawn from from the shelled area.

PROGRAMME OF 2nd PHASE. ZERO Time 10.30 p.m.
Repeated at 12.15 a.m. & 2.30 a.m.

No.		Time	Ammn.	Target.
11	2" Mortars	0 mins to 5 mins 5 mins to 8 mins	25 H.E. 15 H.E.	Front line Trench. Support line Trench.
3	Stokes Mrts	0 mins to 5 mins 5 mins to 10 mins	30 H.E. 30 H.E.	Front line Trench. Flank Barrage.
2	6" Hows.	0 mins to 5 mins 5 mins to 8 mins	8 H.E. 4 H.E.	Front line Trench. Support Trench.
3	4.5" Hows	0 mins to 5 mins 5 mins to 8 mins	30 H.E. 20 H.E.	Front line Trench. Support Trench.
4	18-prs B/162	0 mins to 5 mins	60 H.E. Delay & Shrapnel	Front line Trench.
		5 mins to 10 mins	60 H.E. Delay & Shrapnel	Support Trench.
2	18-prs C/156	7 mins to 10 mins	30 Shrap.	Enfilading Trenches.
4	18-prs B/156 and C/162	0 mins to 10 mins	50 H.E. & Shrap.	Barrage Flanks

SECRET.

Copy   I S

CUINCHY Group, R.F.A.

A bombardment of enemy's trenches 150 yards South of LA Bassee Road will be carried out on May 23rd and May 24th.

At 4 p.m. May 23rd, fire will be directed on to his front line trenches in order to damage them.

All troops are to be clear of front line and saps between BOYAU 26 (inclusive) to BOYAU 32 (inclusive) by 3.45 p.m. Sap 4 to be included. Trench from junction of SHORT CUT and BACK STREET to head of BOYAU 26 (including the Boyau) also to be clear.

At 10.30 p.m. 23rd Instant, 21.15 a.m. and 2.30 a.m. 24th instant, enemy's front line will be bombarded so as to cause loss to parties repairing damaged parapets.

By 10.15 p.m., 12.0 midnight 23rd and 2.15 a.m. 24th all troops will be clear of front line and saps from junction of front line and Boyau running immediately South of WINDMILL (Boyau 28)(inclusive) to Boyau 32 (inclusive) SAP 4 to be included.

Troops can return to front line and saps at 11 p.m. 23rd, 12.45 a.m. and 3.0 a.m. 24th.

Company Commanders concerned will report direct to O.C., CUINCHY Group R.F.A. at DEAD MAN'S HOUSE at 10.15 p.m. and 12 midnight 23rd and 2.15 a.m. 24th and state that all the necessary trenches are clear.

Detailed verbal instructions will be issued to O.C., 1/4th SUFFOLK REGIMENT at 10.30 a.m. 23rd instant.

BMO/594
23rd May, 1916

(SD) R.M.WATSON, Captain
Brigade Major 98th (Infy) Bde.

156 Bde RFA.

When putting away June 1916

Please inform me

H A Cowdery

26. x. 27

A it turned out, the direction selected for the French offensive, towards Becelaere - Zonnebeke - Passchendaele, did not prove fortunate. Apart from the fact that the ridge is practically double here, if not treble, for the Becelaere - Molenhoek - Keiberg spur forms a second crest behind the main one, and Zerhand-Moorslede a third ~~one~~ - the ground was more open then elsewhere, though well dotted with small copses and isolated houses, admirable for the supporting points and machine-gun nests of the defence. Further, the northern part of the Ypres ridge, north of Passchendaele and thence southward along the crest to Broodseinde (east of Zonnebeke) and thence along the bifurcation to Becelaere, was already in the hands of the enemy, and it offered splendid possibilities for observation and defence. It was obvious that this part of the ridge must be re-conquered before any progress could be hoped for. Except a small portion near Broodseinde, none of it was re-taken in 1914.

APPENDIX. I

to 100th Inf Bde
33rd Divnl Arty

"D" 1/10,000.

INSTRUCTIONS FOR ENTERPRISE NIGHT OF 27/28th JUNE 1916.

---

1. The Glasgow Highlanders will raid the hostile craters, front line, support line, and boyaux in the vicinity of MAD POINT A.28.c.9.1.

2. The Tunnelling Company R.E., will destroy mine shafts located in or near the craters.

3. Batteries will co-operate as follows :-
Preliminary Bombardment- 3 minutes.

B/167th.	4 Guns on barrage lines.	H E.
C/166th.	2 guns enfilade from A.28.c.5.5. to A.28.c.9.1.	Shrapnel.
B/166th.	2 guns enfilade from A.28.c.9.2. to A.28.d.3.1.	Shrapnel.
D/166th.	2 guns RAILWAY POINT.	H.E.
	1 Howitzer on MAD POINT Craters.	Ballistite.
	5 Howitzers on lines as in (4)	H.E.

Rates of fire.

Zero to 0.3.
18-pounders-4 rounds per gun per minute.
1-4.5"How: (on craters)-2 rounds per Howitzer per minute.
5-4.5"How:- 1 round per Howitzer per minute.

4. **Barrage :-**

(B/167th.	A.28.c.85.65.	Shrapnel.
(	A.28.d.15.60.	½ Shrapnel. ½.H.E.
(Enfilade up and down LANE ALLEY. East of Railway.		½ Shrapnel. ½.H.E.
(Enfilade up and down MAD ALLEY, East of Railway.		½ Shrapnel. ½.H.E.
(B/166th.	A.28.c.98.52.	H.E.
(	A.28.c.5.6.	½.Shrapnel. ½.H.E.
(Enfilade A.28.d.60.95. to the East.		Shrapnel.
(Telephone lines. A.29.c.45.75.		½.Shrapnel. ½.H.E.
(A/166th.	A.28.c.3.8.	H.E.
	A.28.d.20.75.	½.Shrapnel. ½.H.E.
(C/166th.	Enfilade A.28.c.8.5 .65. to the South East; Enfilade A.28.d.35.25. keeping south of, road.	Shrapnel.
(D/166th.	A.28.c.85.65.; A.28.d.40.15.; A.28.d.90.75.; A.28.d.60.95.; A.28.b.20.25.	H.E.

Rates of fire-18-pounders.

3 rounds per gun per minute.(0.3.to0.8. and 0.58.to 1.3.)
2 rounds per gun per minute (0.8.to0.58.)

4.5"Howitzers.

1 round per How.per minute (0.3. to 1.3.)
Batteries will continue firing at the slower rate, 2 rounds per gun per minute until the order to stop is given.

Continued on page 2.

Continued.

5. will be the forward artillery control at where he will be in communication with Glasgow Highlanders.

6. The 2" Trench Mortars will co-operate according to special instructions issued to D.T.M.O.

7. Zero will be communicated to all Units from Sub-Group Headquarter's Watches will be synchronised .

8. 15th.Division will bombard front line trenches between C.4.B.Central and A.28.d.3.1.

WAR
DIARY

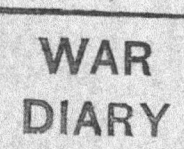

Headquarters,

156th BRIGADE, R.F.A.

(33rd Division)

J U L Y

1 9 1 6

Attached:

Appendices 1 & 2.

JULY. 1916. Sheet 1. 33 July Vol 6

Army Form C. 2118.

Instructions regarding War Diaries and Intelligence Summaries are contained in F. S. Regs., Part II. and the Staff Manual respectively. Title pages will be prepared in manuscript.

WAR DIARY 156th Brigade R.F.A.

or

~~INTELLIGENCE SUMMARY.~~

(Erase heading not required.)

Place	Date	Hour	Summary of Events and Information	Remarks and references to Appendices
GIVENCHY	1.7.16	-	The Brigade remained in action in the same positions as in the latter end of the preceding month. - Wagon lines also remained in the same places as before.	
	1.7.16 to 5.7.16	-	Wire cutting was carried out north & south of the LA BASSÉE Canal at four different points, broad lanes being cut in every place. Daily bombardments of about an hour's duration took place, with a view to deceiving the enemy as to at what point the attack that was to be made on July 5th would take place.	
	5.7.16	10.15p	A raid by the 2nd R.W. Fusiliers was made on SUNKEN TRENCH and East of the DUCK'S BILL CRATERS. The bombardment commenced at 10.15p.m. 6,000 18pr. rounds being fired by Givenchy Group during the 2½ hours that the troops remained in the enemy trenches.	Appendix 1.
	6.7.16.	-	Orders were received that the Brigade was to move and at 8p.m. relief by sections of the 61st Div. Arty. commenced.	
	7.7.16.	-	The Brigade moved out of the firing line to HINGETTE, remaining there one night.	
	9.7.16	3.a.	The Brigade commenced entraining at FOUQUEREUIL, in four trains: the first train	

JULY 1916.

Instructions regarding War Diaries and Intelligence Summaries are contained in F. S. Regs., Part II. and the Staff Manual respectively. Title pages will be prepared in manuscript.

WAR DIARY

or

~~INTELLIGENCE~~ SUMMARY.

(Erase heading not required.)

156th Brigade R.F.A.

Sheet No 2.

Army Form C. 2118.

Place	Date	Hour	Summary of Events and Information	Remarks and references to Appendices
	9.7.16	(contd)	arrived at LONGEAU near AMIENS at 2pm. The head of the column then proceeded to CARDONETTE, about 8 miles N.E. from AMIENS., where the Brigade bivouacked for the night.	
	10.7.16	12 noon	Orders were received for the Brigade to march to HANGEST-SUR-SOMME and the Brigade immediately got on the move, arriving at HANGEST at 9.45 p.m. Headquarter Staff & B Battery were billeted, the remainder bivouacking on the top of the hill. The remainder of the Divisional Artillery were billeted at CROUY & SOUEZ.	
	12.7.16	1.30pm	The Brigade moved to CORBIE, about 25 miles E. of HANGEST, arriving there at 10pm. The horse lines & gun parks were in the Cavalry Park, where the troops bivouacked.	
	13.7.16	6.am	The Brigade marched out of CORBIE & proceeded to bivouac in MARETT WOOD near MERICOURT, where orders were received that ~~the~~ Brigade was under 30 minutes notice to take up position in the line.	
	14.7.16	12 noon	The Brigade marched with the 19th Infantry Brigade in rear of the 1st Cameronians to MEAULTE, where it bivouacked near the River ANCRE, moving again at 6pm to a bivouac half a mile East of the village, where the night was spent.	
	15.7.16	3.am	The Brigade marched in rear of the 19th Infantry Brigade, passing through the old German line at FRICOURT at 6.15 am.	

JULY 1916.

Instructions regarding War Diaries and Intelligence Summaries are contained in F. S. Regs., Part II. and the Staff Manual respectively. Title pages will be prepared in manuscript.

WAR DIARY

or

~~INTELLIGENCE~~ ~~SUMMARY.~~

(Erase heading not required.)

156th Brigade R.F.A.

Sheet 3.

Army Form C. 2118.

Place	Date	Hour	Summary of Events and Information	Remarks and references to Appendices
MAMETZ WOOD	15.7.16.	8 am	A halt was made in the valley while Battery Positions were reconnoitred, the	
	16.-17.7.16	12 mdt.	156th Bde & the 19th Inf. Bde being then in Reserve. B. C. & D Batteries took up positions at the following points, S.14.B.5.4. BAZENTIN-LE-GRAND WOOD, BAZENTIN-LE-GRAND village, and S.14.B.5.6 respectively, supporting the 98th Infantry Brigade in attacks on HIGH WOOD.	
	17.7.16.		'A' Battery came into action at S.20.A.48. Owing to the fact that the whole of HIGH WOOD was not captured by our Infantry, 'C' Battery received orders to withdraw to S.20 A.9.9. Brigade Headquarters were at S.14.A.7.3.	
	21.7.16.	8. am	'D' Battery changed its position and came into action at S.20.A.8.4. Headquarter	
	22.7.16	1 am	Staff also moved to S.20.A.8.4. 'B' Battery moved to S.14.A.9½.9½.	
	23.7.16.		The 33rd Divisional Artillery became CORPS TROOPS owing to fact that the 33rd Divisional Infantry were withdrawn from the line on or about that date. On this date all the wagon-lines were heavily shelled and were ordered to go back to F.2.C. behind FRICOURT.	

July. 1916.

Instructions regarding War Diaries and Intelligence Summaries are contained in F. S. Regs., Part II. and the Staff Manual respectively. Title pages will be prepared in manuscript.

WAR DIARY 156th Brigade R.F.A.

or

~~INTELLIGENCE SUMMARY.~~

(Erase heading not required.)

Sect. 4. Army Form C. 2118.

Place	Date	Hour	Summary of Events and Information	Remarks and references to Appendices
	14.7.16.		'B' Battery & 'D' Battery did a little registration but were unable to fire much until the Infantry had taken the high ground by HIGH WOOD.	
	15.7.16		'A' Battery, & 'C' Battery, registered during the morning from their new positions, 'B' Battery & 'D' Battery doing likewise later in the day from their original positions.	
	19-20.7.16.		At 1. am 20.7.16. the Brigade took part in an attack on HIGH WOOD and the entrenchments running to the N.W. 2000 18pr. rounds & 400 4.5" How. rounds were expended by the Brigade during the bombardment. During the rest of the day an almost continual barrage was kept up to allow the Infantry to consolidate. In the evening, however, the Infantry ~~was compelled to withdraw to their old line~~ established themselves at the bottom of the wood.	Appendix. 2.
	23.7.16		The 51st Division relieved the 33rd Division (less Artillery) and another bombardment & attack was carried out on HIGH WOOD. The 33rd Divisional Artillery had now become Corps Artillery: the 156th Brigade covered the left zone* of the Corps front. The Brigade was no longer directly responsible for the protection of the Infantry, but searched the back areas & approaches.	* S.G.R.G.3 to M.33.D.0.2.
	23-27.7.16.		During this period the ordinary day & night firing was carried out, i.e. 2000 rounds by day & 625 rounds by night	

July. 1916.

Sheet 5.

WAR DIARY 158th Brigade R.F.A.

or

~~INTELLIGENCE SUMMARY.~~

(Erase heading not required.)

Army Form C. [illegible]18.

Instructions regarding War Diaries and Intelligence Summaries are contained in F. S. Regs., Part II. and the Staff Manual respectively. Title pages will be prepared in manuscript.

Place	Date	Hour	Summary of Events and Information	Remarks and references to Appendices
	23-27.7.16	(contd)	with the exception of two occasions on which the Brigade assisted in concentrated bombardments, together with the Heavy Artillery, on portions of the German line in and about HIGH WOOD.	
	28.7.16		From 5.10 am. to 8.10 am. the Brigade took part in a bombardment of the German trench between HIGH WOOD & DELVILLE WOOD. About 1500 18pr. rounds and 400 4.5" Howitzer rounds were expended, mostly on the back area & approaches.	

T2134. Wt. W708-776. -500000. 4/15. Sir J. C. & S.

JULY. 1916.

Instructions regarding War Diaries and Intelligence Summaries are contained in F. S. Regs., Part II. and the Staff Manual respectively. Title pages will be prepared in manuscript.

WAR DIARY

or

[redacted]

(*Erase heading not required.*)

156th Brigade R.F.A. Sheet 6.

Army Form C. 2118.

Place	Date	Hour	Summary of Events and Information	Remarks and references to Appendices
	17.7.16		Capt. R.D. RUSSELL, 2.Lt. RA. GREENWOOD, 2.Lt. P.G. WOODRUFFE were wounded, and 2.Lt. H. BALDWIN was killed, all of 'B' Battery. 2 Lt. T.D. CHALLEN of 'A' Battery was also evacuated. On this date Lt. & Adjt. W.G. PRINGLE was posted temporarily in command of B. Battery, and 2Lt. B.L. OXLEY, the Orderly Officer, became Acting Adjutant in his place.	
	20.7.16		Up to this date the casualties in the Brigade were 3 N.C.O's & 8 men wounded. On this date 2.Lt. W. BARLOW of 'A' Battery was wounded.	
	23.7.16		Up to this date the casualties in the Brigade were 2 N.C.O's & 7 men killed, 1 N.C.O & 11 men wounded. On this date 2.Lt. L.H. WHITE of 'C' Battery was wounded.	
	26.7.16		Up to this date the casualties in the Brigade were 2 N.C.O's & 6 men killed, 4 N.C.O's & 13 men wounded. On this date 2Lt. L.A.S. PRIOR of 'B' Battery was killed.	
	28.7.16.		A draft of 2 FITTERS, 5 signallers & 12 gunners arrived.	
	29.7.16		2.Lt. J. I[redacted]. WATSON arrived and was posted to 'B' Battery.	
	31.7.16		Up to this date the casualties in the Brigade were 2 men killed, 1 N.C.O. & 3 men wounded. Total Casualties for the month, 2 Officers killed & 6 wounded, 9 N.C.O's killed & 4 wounded, 15 men killed & 35 wounded.	

T2134. Wt. W708—776. 500000. 4/15. Sir J. C. & S.

H. Rochfort-Boyd Lt Col.

A P P E N D I C E S 1 & 2 .

SECRET. Copy No 1 33 D.A 2 19th I.B 3 RE AWF No 4 Office 5 D.A 6 7 19th I.B. — Office Copy No 4

APPENDIX I.

GIVENCHY GROUP.

1. On the night of 5/6th July the 19th Infantry Brigade will carry out an attack with the object of capturing and consolidating the enemy's front line between A9B19.43 and A9B 35.06 holding it with flanks joined to our present system.

2. Timings: Zero will be notified later.

0.0. to 0.45	Artillery and T.M. Bombardment - between A9B19.43 and A9B 35.06
0.35	Mine blown at about A22 A 28 Gas - Smoke - & Artillery Barrage (c) lasting till 1.15
0.45	Attack Bombardment changes to Barrage.
0.50	Mine blown at about A9D 8.4. Artillery Barrage (b) lasting till 1.25

3. The Artillery support will consist of -

(a) Preparation of main attack and Barrage during consolidation.

No attention will have been drawn to the spot previous to zero time except for wire cutting similar to that carried out at other points in the line.

The fire programme of the 3 pricipal 18-pr Batteries, the Howitzers and Mortars attached.

The left flank is covered by B/184 (4 guns), who fire on trenches between A9B69 and A3D64

0.0. to 1 hour at $1\frac{1}{2}$ rounds per gun per minute
1 hour to 2 hours at 1 round per gun per minute

The right flank is covered by C/162 who fire on trenches between A9D85 65 and A9D 85 90.

0.0. to 1 hour at 2 rounds per gun per minute (4 guns)
1 hour to 2 hours at 1 round per gun per minute "
They also join in (b)

(b) Feint attack and Barrage on the explosion of a mine at about A9D84 at 0.50

C/162 (2 guns)) 0.50 to 0.55 3 rounds per gun per minute.
A/167 (4 guns)) Fire is then lifted.
) 0.55 to 1.25 2 rounds per gun per minute.

(c) Feint attack and Barrage on the explosion of a mine at about A22A28 at 0.35 in conjunction with gas and smoke.

B/156 (6 guns) 0.35 to 1.15, 3 rounds per gun per minute
D/156 50 rounds.

4. From 0.0. to 2 hours the estimated expenditure of ammunition is as follows unless a strong counter attack is made by the Germans :-

18-prs	6000
4.5" Hows	1200
6" Hows	30
2" Mortars	600
Stokes	3000

5. After 2 hours the expenditure of ammunition will depend on the success of the consolidation, and the German counter offensive.

Programme for A/162
Enfilade 4 18pm

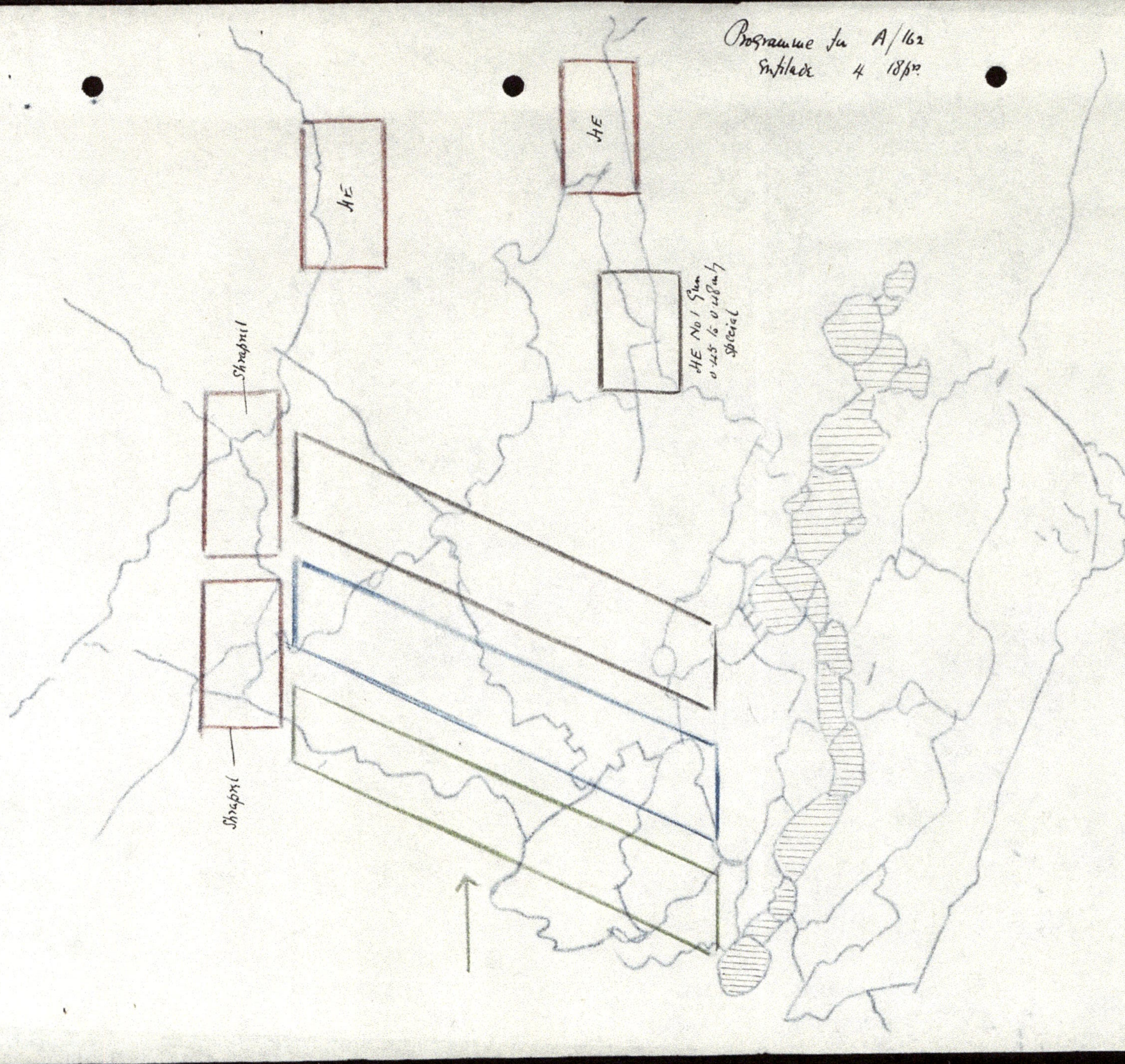

Time Table

00	to	0.10	Green	} half HE half Shrapnel
10	to	17	Blue	
17	to	20	Brown	
20	to	30	Green	
30	to	33	Brown	
33	to	40	Blue	} HE
40	to	45	Green	
45	to	48	Brown special	
48	to	2hrs.	Red	

Rate of Fire

00 to 1 hours 3 Rounds per Gun per min
1 hour to 2 hours 2 " " " " "

Total 1200

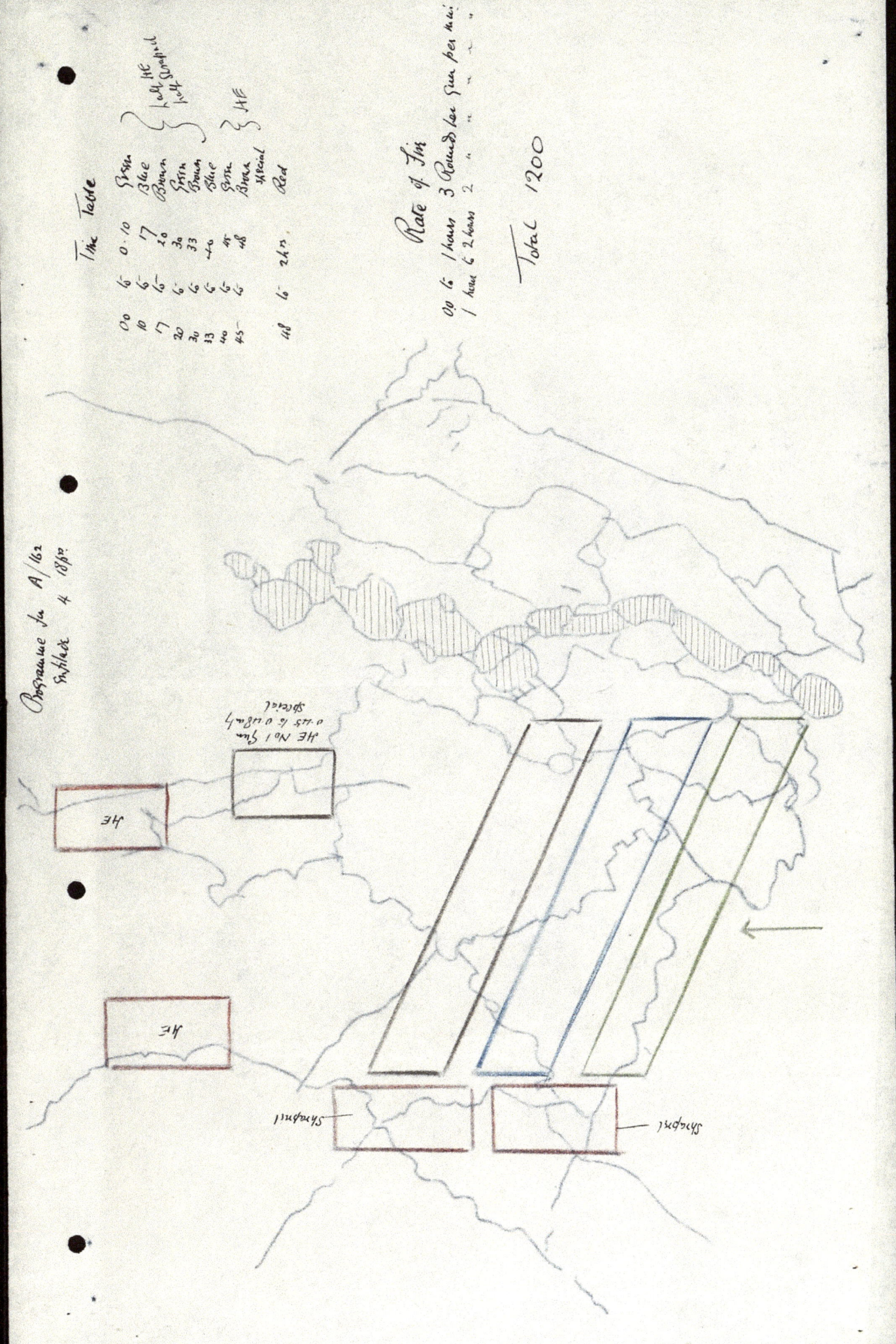

Programme of A 56 Enfilade (2.18 p.m.)

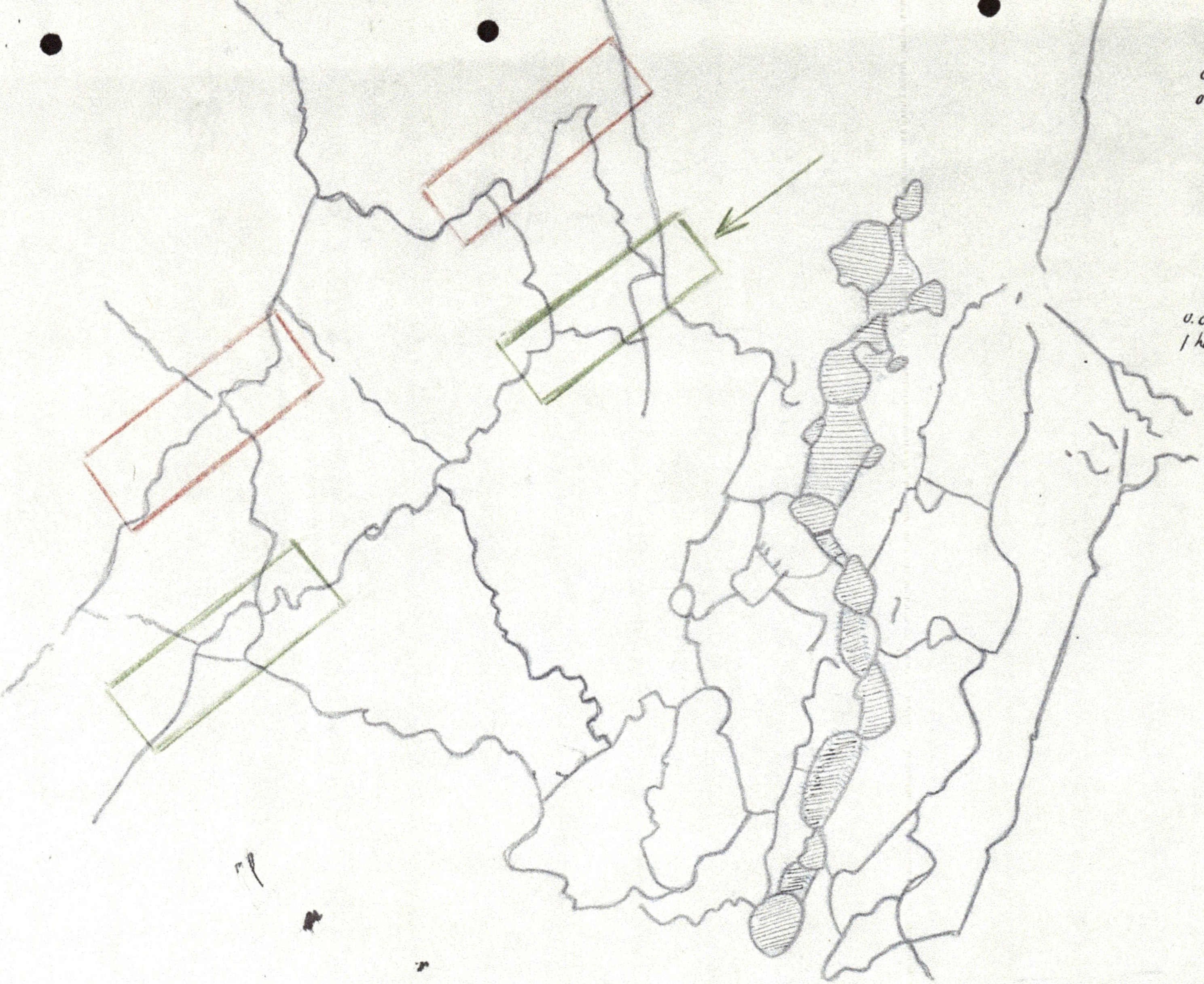

Time Table

0.0 to 0.48 Green
0.48 to 2 hours Red

~~HE & Half~~ Shrapnel (only)

Rate of Fire

0.0 to 1 hr. 3 Rounds per gun per min
1 hour to 2 hours 2 " " " " "

Total 600

Programme for Howitzers

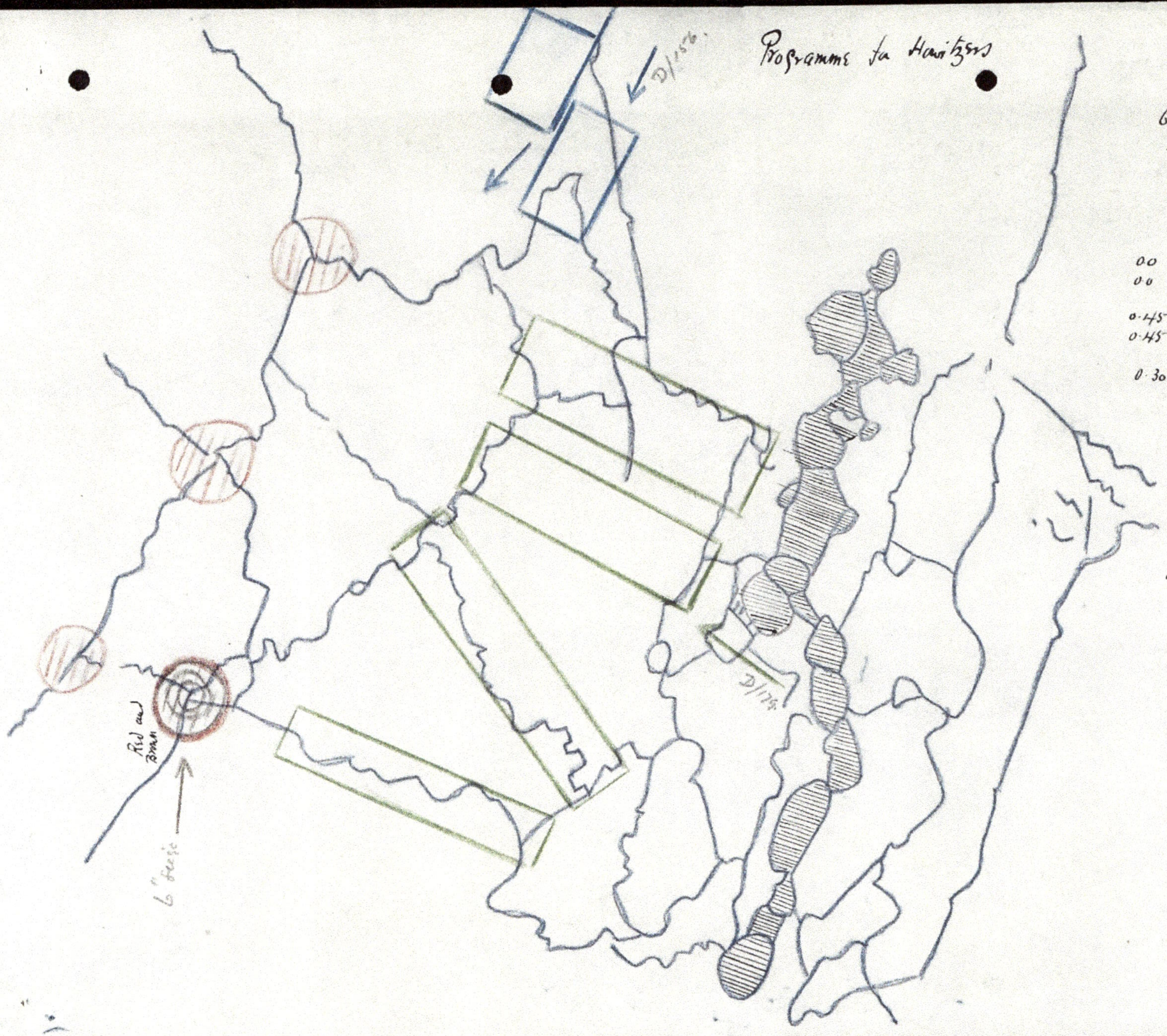

D/179 4 Hows'
D/156 1½ Hows
6" Siege 2 Hows

Time Table

0.0 to 0.45	D/179	Green
0.0 to 0.45	D/156	Blue
0.45 to 2 hrs	D/179	Red
0.45 to 2 hrs	D/156	Continues same locality
0.30 to 1.30	6" Siege	Brown

Rate of Fire 4.5s

0.0 to 0.60	2 Rounds per how. per min
0.60 to 2 hours	1½ " " " " "

Total

4.5"	1260
6" Siege	30

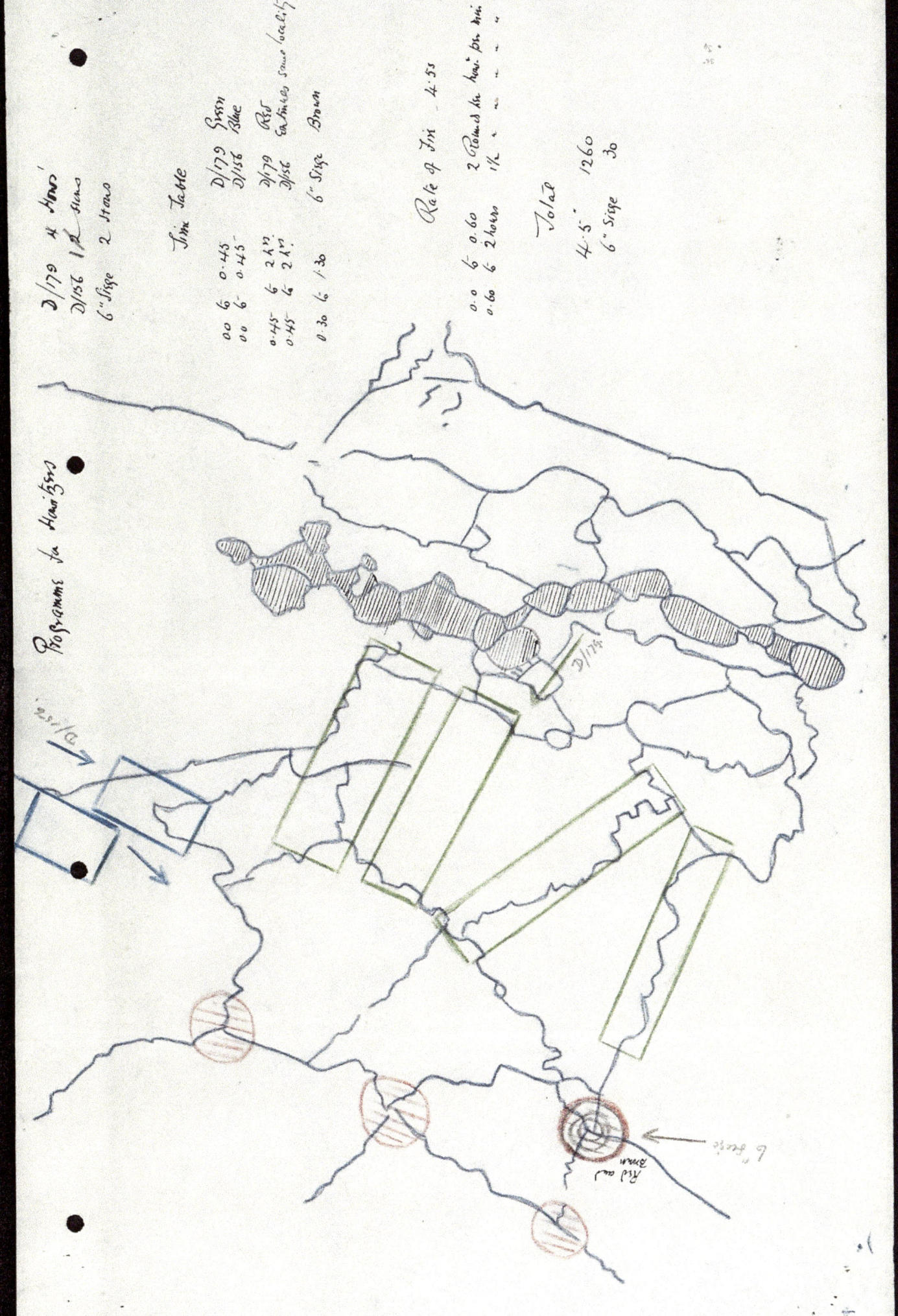

Programme of C/86 Frontal Fire
4 - 18 p.

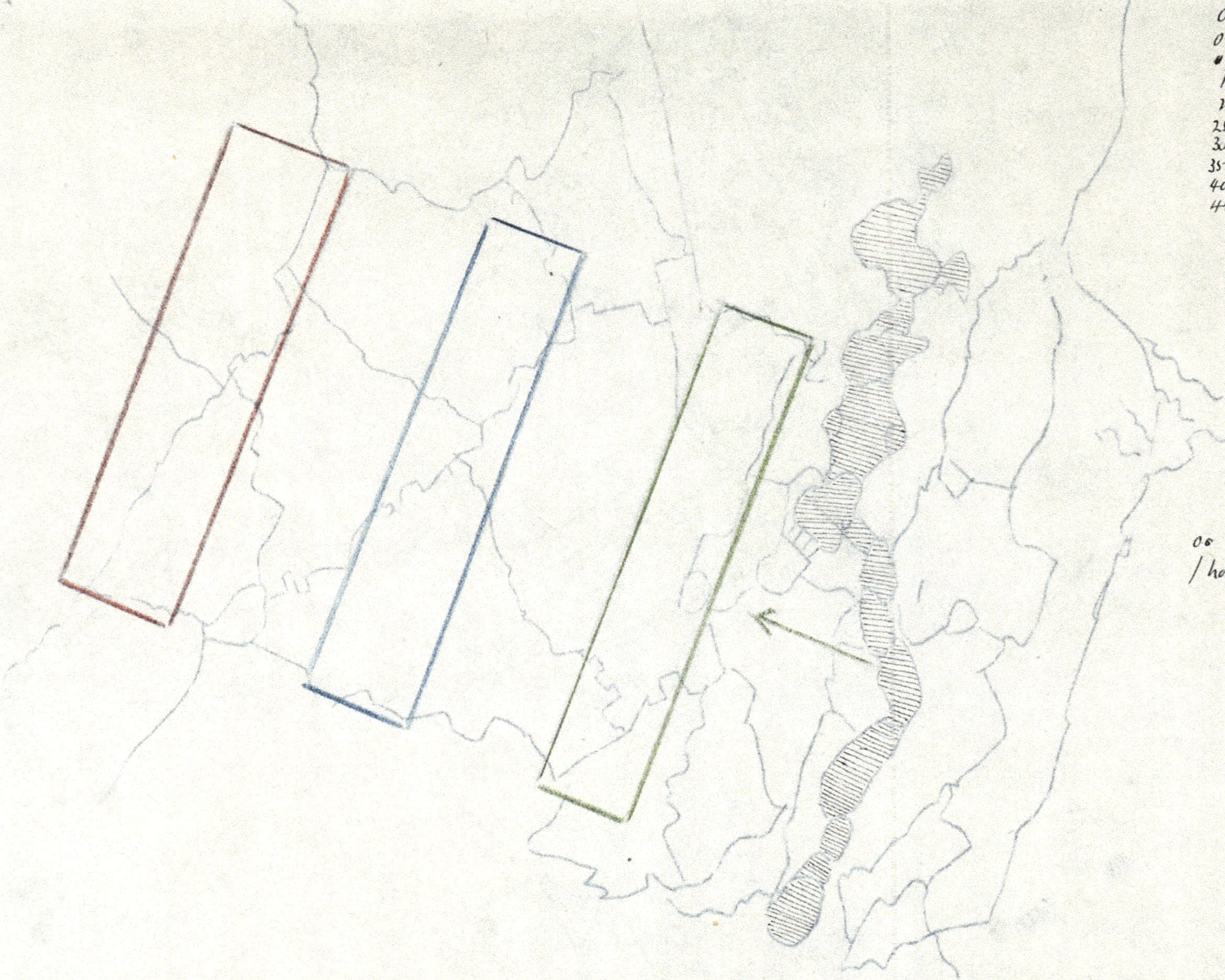

Time Table

0.0 to 0.5	Green	Half HE Half Shrapnel	
0.5 to 0.10	Blue		
0.10 to 0.15	Green		
15 to 20	Blue		
20 to 25	Green		
25 to 30	Blue	HE	
30 to 35	Green		
35 to 40	Blue		
40 to 45	Green		
45 to Slacken Fire	Red	All Shrapnel	

Rate of Fire

00 to 1 hour 3 Rds per Gun Per min
1 hour to 2 hours 2 " " " "

Total 1200

Stokes Mortars

(12).

Zones 0.01–0.45

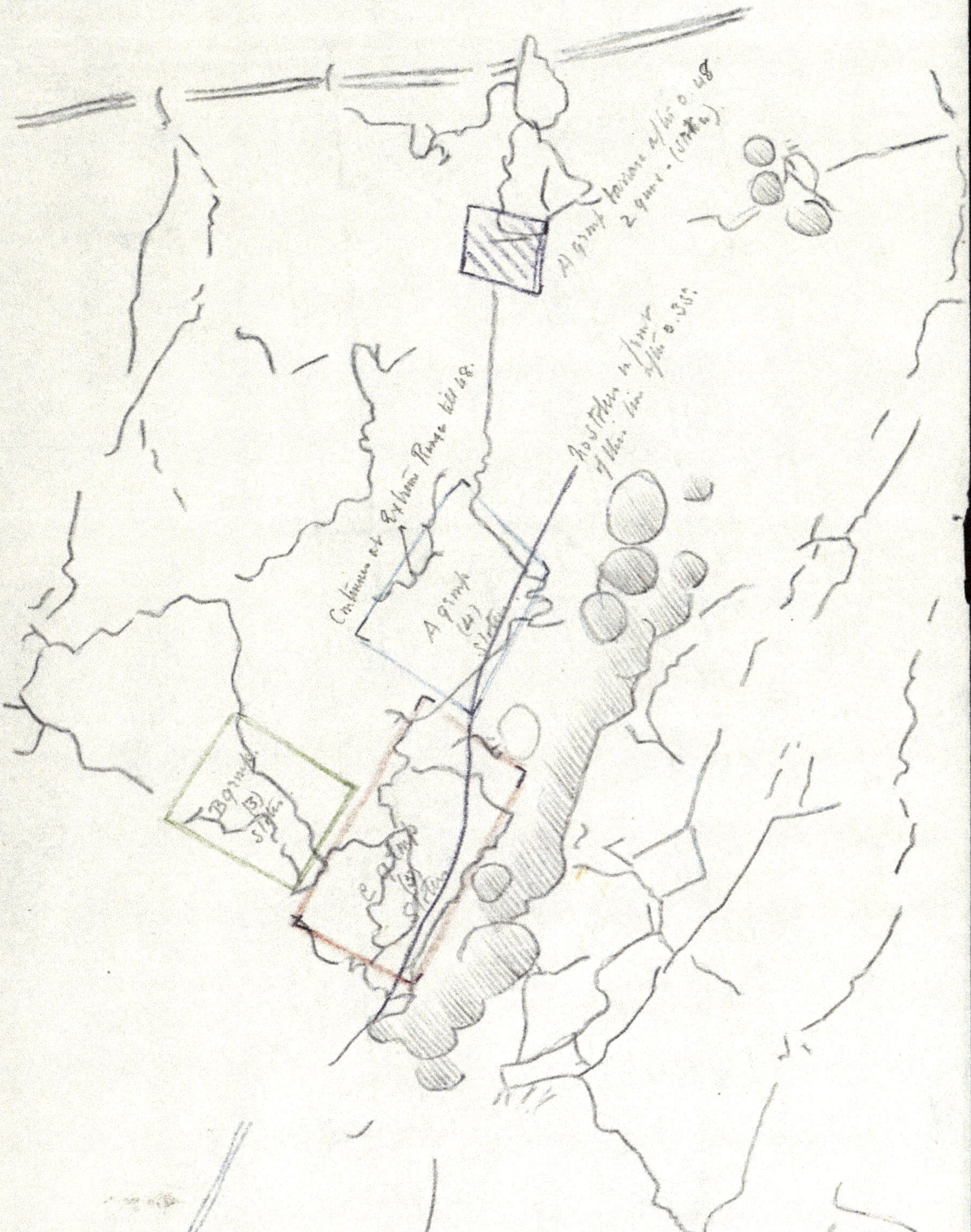

2" Mortars (12)

Zones 0.0 to 0.45

Barrage after 0.45 shaded

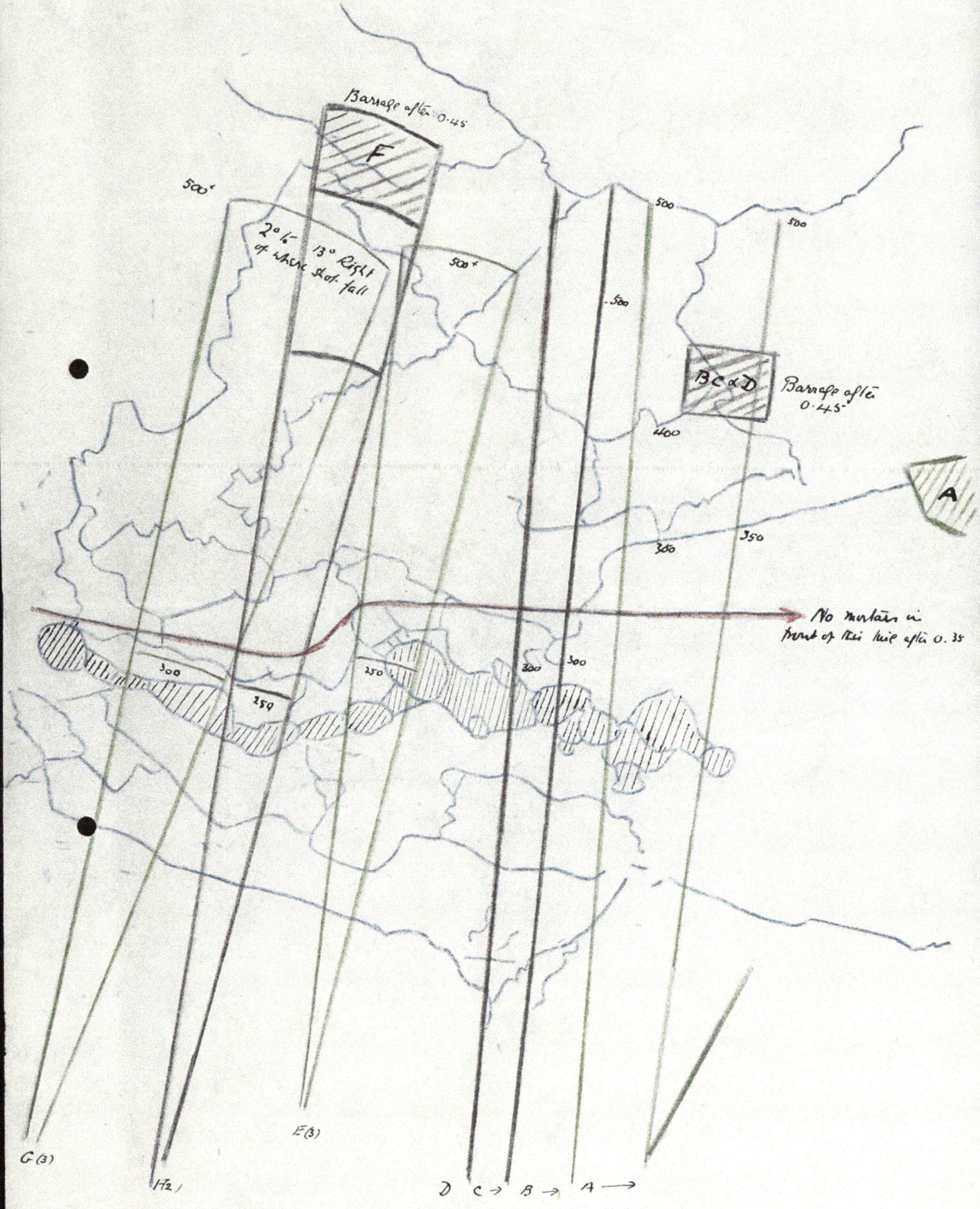

E GROUP ceases fire at 0.45 unless forward platoon is driven in

G GROUP switch maximum to LEFT & fire smoke bombs at 500*

G.O.C.
33rd Division.

A.11
33rd Div.

XI Corps R.H.S. 1137.

I wish you to convey to all ranks in your Division my great appreciation of the successful operations they have carried out during the time they have been in the Corps, operations which have received frequently the approbation of the General Officer Commanding the First Army, and of the Commander-in-Chief.

The many raids that have been undertaken by the 33rd Division have furnished models for other Divisions, newly arrived from England to join the Corps, and the two recently carried out by the GLASGOW HIGHLANDERS and the ROYAL WELSH FUSILIERS respectively, have shewn a brilliance in design and gallantry in execution which could not be surpassed.

I have to thank all ranks for the ready response that they have made whenever I have called upon them to undertake any offensive operations. I have found a fine fighting spirit throughout the Division at all times, and it ~~ism~~ with the greatest regret that I have to say "Good-bye".

I have seen and spoken to nearly all the Officers, and to many of the N.C.Os and men of the Division, and I shall regret your departure more than that of of any of the sixteen Divisions that have been in my Corps since it was formed, because you areall such fine fighting soldiers.

I wish you 'God speed and victory', and I hope before the end of the war I may again have the high honour of including the 33rd Division in the XIth Corps under my Command.

9/7/16.

(Sd)R.HAKING, Lieut-General,
Commanding XIth Corps.

ALL UNITS, 33rd Division.

It gives the G.O.C. great pleasure to forward to you, for communication to all ranks, the above copy of a letter received from Lieut.General Sir R.HAKING, Commanding XIth Corps.

10/7/16

(Sd)F.S CUMMINGS, Lt-Col
A.A.& Q.M.G. 33rd Division

FILE

S E C R E T. APPENDIX 2

33 DA
BM/S/458

O.C.

156 Brigade, R.F.A.

1. Zones of Brigades are Right to Left

Left		Left Centre	Right Centre	Right
156th Bde.	&	166th Bde.	167th Bde.	162nd Bde.

2. Up to 100 rounds a gun and 75 rounds per 4.5" howitzer } may be used during the bombardment up to the final barrage.

3. The last ten minutes before the assault will be intense.

4. Zero to 0.30 Section Fire 30 seconds.

0.30 to 0.60 Section Fire 1 minute.

~~0.60 till further orders~~.

5. Please acknoeledge by wire to Advance Headquarters 33rd Div. Arty.

6. Zero time to be obtained from Infantry but may be checked from Div Arty if telephone lines hold.

F.K. Sadler. Major, R.A..

19.7.16. Brigade Major 33rd Divisional Artillery.

2. 5.55 [illegible] 3 secs. Sec per ~~30 sec~~. 2 rounds a min. 60 ~~[illegible]~~ rounds an hour.

3. 5

3. 15 am Quicken 1 sec per 15 secs.

SECRET. 15 C.A.10/156.

ARRANGEMENTS FOR NIGHT FIRING.

1. During the night of 19th-20th July.-

   (i) Up to the hour for the commencement of the bombardment the arrangements for night firing and the allotment of ammunition will be the same as for last night.

   (ii) After the final barrage the zones will be as in XVth Corps Artillery Operation Order No. 24 of today's date.

2. Acknowledge.

19.7.16.

Sd. J.M.R. Harrison, Major,
Staff Officer to B.G. R.A. XV Corps.

SECRET.

XV CORPS ARTILLERY OPERATION ORDER No. 24.

July 19th.

Reference 1/20,000 Map MARTINPUICH
and Barrage Map X2 attached.

1. The XV Corps will attack on the morning of the 20th July and establish themselves on a line running approximately from S.17.a.4.2 North along Road to about S.11.c.0.4 - thence to S.11.c.5.9 - North West along road to East Corner of HIGH WOOD - North East edge of HIGH WOOD - North West edge of HIGH WOOD to SWITCH TRENCH - North West along SWITCH TRENCH to S.4.a.0.7 - South West along Trench to S.3.b.6.4 - South East along Road to West Corner of HIGH WOOD - thence along road to NORTH of BAZENTIN-LE-PETIT.

2. The bombardment will commence at 2.55 a.m.

3. The hour of zero will be 3.25 a.m.

4. The XIIIth Corps will assist by firing on strong points North of LONGUEVAL VILLAGE.

5. (a) The 7th Divisional Artillery will be responsible for bombarding all the area South East of HIGH WOOD and the South East edge of the WOOD and for barraging SWITCH TRENCH East of HIGH WOOD.
The G.O.C. 7th Divisional Artillery will make the necessary arrangements for the above.

(b) The G.O.C. 33rd Divisional Artillery will concentrate the whole of his 18pounders and 4.5" howitzers on HIGH WOOD and the Trenches North West of the WOOD that are to be taken.

(c) The G.O.C. 21st Divisional Artillery will concentrate one Brigade on HIGH WOOD.
The remainder of his batteries should be employed on SWITCH TRENCH West of HIGH WOOD and in searching the ground on both sides of SWITCH TRENCH, especially the Southern Side. His 4.5" Howitzers should be employed on SWITCH TRENCH between HIGH WOOD and M.33.c.7.3.

(d) The G.O.C. Heavy Artillery will detail as many heavy howitzer batteries as possible to bombard HIGH WOOD, the trenches to be attacked just North West of the WOOD and SWITCH TRENCH for 400 or 500 yards on either side of the WOOD.
He will also detail as many 60 pounders as can be spared to assist in the attack on the Roads South of HIGH WOOD and to sweep the ground immediately North East of these Roads.

6. (a) At 3 minutes before zero all Howitzers will search back to a line - West edge of LONGUEVAL VILLAGE to road junction at S.11.c.5.8 - along Road to S.4.d.5.4 - thence to point S.4.d.1.4 - straight across HIGH WOOD to S.4.a.2.4 - thence along SWITCH TRENCH.
The 12" howitzers will turn on to MARTINPUICH.
At zero all 18pounders and 60 pounders will do the same

(b) At 7 minutes after zero all howitzers except those on SWITCH TRENCH outside the WOOD, will search back for a distance of 150 yards beyond the line to be attacked, when they will cease firing.
Howitzers on SWITCH TRENCH will continue for half-an-hour, but will not fire closer to HIGH WOOD than 300 yards on the East side and 600 on the NORTH WEST side.

At 10 minutes after zero all 18 pounders and 60 pounders on the line to be attacked will search back for 500 yards.

(c) The G.O.C. 7th Divisional Artillery will find out from the left Division of the XIIIth Corps how far South it is safe for his guns to fire. He will not fire South of S.11 Central unless asked to do so by the XIIIth Corps.

7. A barrage will be immediately established and continue for one hour, after which the usual night firing will be resumed.

LIMITS OF BARRAGE.

7th Divisional Artillery from Junction with XIIIth Corps to S.4.b.5.3

33rd Divisional Artillery.from S.4.b.5.3 inclusive to ~~Mx33xdx5x0~~ M.33.d.5.0 inclusive.

21st Divisional Artillery from M.33.d.5.0 to left of XV Corps.

All ground over which the enemy can advance should be well searched at frequent intervals.

The Heavy Artillery will search more distant approaches and Villages.

8. During the bombardment and 1st Lift the fire should be fairly heavy and in each case the last five minutes intense.

18 pounders firing on HIGH WOOD should use H.E. mostly except on the front edge of the WOOD and for 2 or 3 minutes before each Lift.

9. Points to which special attention should be paid are :-

The 4 corners of HIGH WOOD.
New trench just North of HIGH WOOD.
S.4.a.35.20.
SWITCH TRENCH where it runs through the WOOD and for 500 yards North West.
SUNKEN ROAD for a distance of 50 yards North of WOOD.

10. Acknowledge.

Sd. J.M.R. Harrison, Major,
S.O. to B.G. R.A. XV Corps.

19th July, 1916.

S E C R E T.   Copy No. 8

33rd Division Order No.54.

Ref.1/20,000 Map
MARTINPUICH.   18th July 1916.

1. The attack ordered in 33rd Division Order No.52 of 17th inst. will take place tomorrow morning at the hour Zero which will be communicated later.

2. The orders for the attack given in the above mentioned Division Order hold good for tomorrow.
   The dividing line for assembly purposes has been communicated under 33rd Div. G.278 of 17th inst.

3. On 19th July the bombardment will quicken up from 10 minutes before Zero until 5 minutes before Zero, when it will become intense.

4. The hour of Zero will be communicated by following telegram :-

"Bus leaves AMIENS (hour of Zero)."

B Pakenham Major
G.S.
33rd Division.

Issued at 11.~~45~~ 30 a.m.

Copies to :-

1. G.O.C.	13. C.R.E.
2) File.	14. A.D.M.S.
3)	15. 98 Inf.Bde.
4. A.A & Q.M.G.	16. 19 Inf.Bde.
5. C.R.A.	17. 100 Inf.Bde.
6. 5th Divn.	18. Pioneer Bn.
7. Signal Coy.	19. Div. Train.
8. 156 Bde.R.F.A.	20) XV Corps.
9. 162 Bde.R.F.A.	21)
10. 166 Bde.R.F.A.	22. 7th Divn.
11. 167 Bde.R.F.A.	23. 21st Divn.
12. Div.Amm.Col.	

Bm/S/430

15/CA/10/143/1

AMENDMENTS TO INSTRUCTIONS FOR BOMBARDMENT AND BARRAGES.

1. Reference 15 CA 10/143 dated 16th July, 1916, the following amendments are to be made :-

Para. 4 (b) i

"Delete first four lines and substitute -
"At 13 minutes before zero all howitzers on HIGH WOOD and on the "Trench running from West Corner of HIGH WOOD to S.3.b.5.4 will "search back until they arrive at a line running from S.4.d.1.4 to "S.4.a.2.4 and that portion of SWITCH TRENCH behind the Trench from "HIGH WOOD to S.3.b.5.4.
" At 10 minutes before zero all 18 pounders on HIGH WOOD and the "Trench from West corner of the Wood to S.3.b.5.4 will do the same"

Para. 4 (b) ii

Line 1. For "27 minutes" substitute "17 minutes".

Line 3. For "30 minutes" substitute "20 minutes".

~~Paraxxx~~
Para. 6

Delete "For all howitzers and guns the last 5 minutes before zero "will be intense" and substitute -

"The fire of all howitzers and guns will be increased at 10 "minutes before zero and the last 5 minutes will be intense".

2. Acknowledge.

17th July, 1916. Sd. J.M.R. Harrison, Major,
Staff Officer to B.G. R.A. XV Corps.

2.

O.C.

156 Brigade, R.F.A.

1. The bombardment will commence at 1 a.m. ~~19th instant~~.

2. Zero time will probably be about 3.30 a.m.

3. Targets are as shewn in my B.M/S/438 (with amendment of 156th Bde. How. for 167th Bde. How).

4. Ammunition.

18prs. 100 rounds a gun will be used during the bombardment.
4.5" Hows. will fire 75 rounds a gun during the bombardment.

The fire of all howitzers and guns will be increased at 10 minutes before zero and the last five minutes will be intense.

At zero 18prs on SWITCH TRENCH will search back by short lifts for 600 yards after which 33rd D.A. 18prs will continue to search MARTINPUICH and approaches to and from at frequent intervals.

Zero to 0.30 Section fire 30 seconds.
0.30 to 0.60 Section fire 1 minute.
0.60 till further orders. Bursts of fire at intervals.
Ammunition expenditure equivalent to Section fire 2 minutes.

5. 4.5" Howitzers are distributed along trench from HIGH WOOD to M.33.d.0.2 until 3 minutes before zero. They then search back by 50 yards for a distance of 150 yards. After which they search MARTINPUICH and approaches to and from at frequent intervals. Rate of fire equivalent to Section fire 4 minutes.

6. Please acknowledge by wire

8.7.16

Major, R.A.
BRIGADE MAJOR 33RD DIVISIONAL ARTILLERY

33rd Divisional Artillery
;;;;;;;;;;

156th BRIGADE

ROYAL FIELD ARTILLERY

AUGUST 1 9 1 6

Original
156 RFA
Vol 7

CONFIDENTIAL

WAR DIARY

of

156th BDE RFA

from Aug 1st 1916 to Aug 31st 1916

Volume

Instructions regarding War Diaries and Intelligence Summaries are contained in F. S. Regs., Part II. and the Staff Manual respectively. Title pages will be prepared in manuscript.

WAR DIARY

or

INTELLIGENCE SUMMARY.

(Erase heading not required.)

Army Form C. 2118.

Place	Date	Hour	Summary of Events and Information	Remarks and references to Appendices

T2134. Wt. W708—776. 500000. 4/15. Sir J. C. & S.

Instructions regarding War Diaries and Intelligence Summaries are contained in F. S. Regs., Part II. and the Staff Manual respectively. Title pages will be prepared in manuscript.

WAR DIARY
or
~~INTELLIGENCE SUMMARY~~
(Erase heading not required.)

1

156th BDE RFA

Army Form C. 2118.

Place	Date	Hour	Summary of Events and Information	Remarks and references to Appendices
	August		1	
BAZENTIN LE GRAND	1st		The Brigade remained in the line as before under the orders of the GOC XV Corps	
			HQ at S20 A 84 — A Bty S 20 A 48 B Bty S 14 c 90 C Bty S 20 A 99	
			D Bty S 20 A 84 — Wagon lines at F 2 6	
			D Bty was attached to Heavy Arty Group for Counter Battery firing	
			The CRA 51st Div Arty (HQ at F3 B 62 Fricourt) issued tactical instructions	
	1st		Zones allotted were as in Appendix I	Appendix I
	2nd	4 am.	Zone changed to S3 D69 to S3 D05 inclusive.	
			Strong hostile attack on our line N of BAZENTIN LE PETIT successfully repulsed.	
			Heavy hostile shelling of positions and vicinity during the day	
			The Bde was put on an allowance of 400 Rds (18pr) during every night.	
			and 60 Rds per hour during the day time	
	3rd		Capt C/C MAUNSELL took over command of B Bty and LIEUT W.G. PRINGLE returned to HQ.	
	4th	12 30 am.	An attack was made on German Trenches from S11 D 60 75 – S11 D08 – S11 c 58	
			The 51st DA assisted and the 156th Bde fired 400 Rds on the Brigade Zone S4A 32 – S4B 30	
	4th	2 40 am	Normal firing resumed	

2

Instructions regarding War Diaries and Intelligence Summaries are contained in F. S. Regs., Part II. and the Staff Manual respectively. Title pages will be prepared in manuscript.

WAR DIARY
or
~~INTELLIGENCE SUMMARY.~~ 156th Bde RFA
(Erase heading not required.)

Army Form C. 2118.

Place	Date	Hour	Summary of Events and Information	Remarks and references to Appendices
	Aug.			
BAZENTIN	5th	7.45 pm	Our wagon lines were spotted by hostile planes and were shelled by a 4" gun at 9 pm	WP
	"	11.48 pm	The brigade received an SOS Call vicinity of HIGH WOOD & put up a barrage fire till 11.57 pm.	
	6th	4 am	Wagon lines removed to F7c 8.3.	WP
	6th		33rd Div Infantry commenced relief of 51st Div. On their right was the 17th DIV and on the left the III CORPS	WP
			During the week the following OPs were used S16 B 74. S15 C 59. S3 C 90. S2 C 25	
			Arcs of fire – A Bty. S5 Central to S1 Central	
			B – S12 Central to S1 Central	
			C – S12 Central to S1 Central	
			Ammunition expended during the week 5630 Shrapnel. 2000 HE. 1440 4.5 HE.	WP
	7th	4.30 pm	Bombardment of E Corner of HIGH WOOD carried out to assist XIII CORPS operation	Appendix 2
		6.30 pm	NORMAL firing resumed.	
		11 pm	Very heavy hostile shelling of Batteries & vicinity commenced and did not decrease in intensity till	
	8th	2.45 am	when the number of Shells falling showed an appreciable slackening	WP
		3.30 am	Hostile fire became normal – 4 dug outs were blown in 2 gunpits hit	

T2131. Wt. W708–776. 500000. 4/15. Sir J. C. & S.

Instructions regarding War Diaries and Intelligence Summaries are contained in F. S. Regs., Part II. and the Staff Manual respectively. Title pages will be prepared in manuscript.

3

WAR DIARY
or
~~INTELLIGENCE~~ SUMMARY.
(Erase heading not required.)

156th Bde RFA

Army Form C. 2118.

Place	Date	Hour	Summary of Events and Information	Remarks and references to Appendices
SOMME	Aug			
BAZENTIN	8th	4am	We bombarded localities near HIGH WOOD – NORMAL firing resumed at 6 pm	WGP Appendix
			2850 Rounds were fired between 4 pm 7th and 6 am on the following Day –	
	9th		Nothing of note.	
	10th	11.45pm	SOS received from HIGH WOOD. The Brigade barraged until 12.15 am on the 11th	WGP
	11th	12.15am	when the situation was reported as being NORMAL.	WGP
	12th	5pm	The Brigade marched out on relief by the 166th Bde RFA	WGP
		9pm	BIVOUAC at DERNANCOURT	
	13th and		following days the Brigade remained at DERNANCOURT –	WGP
	23rd	8am	The Brigade went in to action, 1 hours interval between each battery – A 167 was attached	WGP
			The following positions were occupied HQ. A2C 9½ 9 · A Bty A3B16	
			B A2B20 C, A3A08 D Bty A2C 9½ 9 and A 167 A3A47	
			The wagon lines were at E12 A.	WGP
MONTAUBAN	24th		A bombardment was carried out in accordance with 7th DA programme	Appendix 3
			in support of 14th DIV, who made a successful advance in DELVILLE WOOD	WGP
	24th	6.30pm	Rate of fire reduced to 120 Rds per Bty per hour	
		10pm	Rate reduced to 120 Rds for the Group and 30 4.5 How per hour	

T2134. Wt. W708–776. 500000. 4/15. Sir J. C. & S.

Instructions regarding War Diaries and Intelligence Summaries are contained in F. S. Regs., Part II. and the Staff Manual respectively. Title pages will be prepared in manuscript.

WAR DIARY
or
INTELLIGENCE SUMMARY.
(Erase heading not required.)

4

156th Bde RFA

Army Form C. 2118.

Place	Date	Hour	Summary of Events and Information	Remarks and references to Appendices
	Aug.			
MONTAUBAN	25	12 am	Rate of fire reduced to 80 Rds per Group (the brigade + A 167 was called D GROUP Lt Col H C Rochfort-Boyd DSO RFA in Command)	
	25th		New positions in A 22 B were reconnoitred in preparation for a bombardment of GINCHY	WP
	26th	8 pm	Sections took over new positions	
	27th	8 pm	D Group HQ and the remaining sections plus B/167 (Major D STEWART RFA) took over the new positions – HQ at S 22 C 79 – A Bty S 22 B 37 B Bty S 22 B 48 C Bty S 23 A 08 D Bty S 22 B 96 – A/167 (Capt S TALBOT RFA) S 22 A 19 – B 167 S 22 A 97 under the orders of 7th D.A.	WP WP
	28th 29th		About 6000 rounds per battery were brought up to the positions in spite of adverse weather conditions – Teams and wagons were obtained from the 33rd DAC and the 7th DAC to assist in this –	WP
	29th	8 am	The bombardment of GINCHY & trenches in that locality commenced but at 3.10 pm the bombardment was cancelled – Normal firing of 30 Rds per battery was resumed –	WP

T2134. Wt. W708–776. 500000. 4/15. Sir J. C. & S.

5

WAR DIARY

or

~~INTELLIGENCE~~ SUMMARY. 156th BDE RFA

(Erase heading not required.)

Army Form C. 2118.

Instructions regarding War Diaries and Intelligence Summaries are contained in F. S. Regs., Part II. and the Staff Manual respectively. Title pages will be prepared in manuscript.

Place	Date	Hour	Summary of Events and Information	Remarks and references to Appendices
SOMME	Aug			
MONTAUBAN	30th		Heavy rain till rendering trenches used as cover for officers and ~~[illegible]~~ staffs and guns pits which had only been hastily constructed almost uninhabitable.	[initials]
	31st	11pm	Thousands of lethal shells fell in the vicinity but the PH & PHG helmets proved efficacious and there were only a few casualties. B 167 suffering somewhat heavily. 3 officers including the OC & second in command and 15 OR being gassed and evacuated.	[initials]
	August		General. No battery was singled out for particular attention by the enemy but on several occasions the shelling was intense. In the early part of the month a large proportion of guns went out of action chiefly owing to Running out springs failing. Deficiencies were made up from other Brigades out at rest while repairs were being effected at the workshops at HEILLY. Casualties 10 OR killed 29 OR wounded. Drafts 81 OR. Evacuations 12 (sick). Posted away 16 OR. General health. Very good. Some diarrhoea during the middle of the month owing to prevalence of flies at DERNANCOURT.	Appendix 4

H. Rochfort-Boyd Lt Col
Cd 156th Bde

T2134. Wt. W708—776. 500000. 4/15. Sir J. C. & S.

Appendix 1

S E C R E T   Copy No. 15

7th Divisional Artillery Operation Order No. 27

- * -

Hd. Qrs. Divnl. Arty.
30th August, 1918.

1. Owing to present weather conditions the French have postponed their attack for 48 hours.
The attack of the Fourth Army is therefore ordered to take place on the 1st September at the same time as the French attack.

2. (a) The Operations ordered in 7th Divisional Artillery Operation Order No.26 of 28th August will be carried out on 1st September instead of 30th August.

(b) The hour of "Zero" will be notified later. It will be approximately at the hour already ordered, forwarded in B.M.12 of 29-8-18.

(c) All other orders for the operations hold good for 1st September, (the dates being adjusted 48 hours), except as follows:-

(1) The preliminary bombardment will commence on 31st August at 8 a.m. There will be no increase in the intensity of the bombardment by heavy or field artillery prior to zero.

(2) Rate of fire of 4.5" howitzers during the preliminary bombardment will be 50 rounds per battery per hour, as laid down in paragraph 7 of Operation Order No.25 dated 26-8-18.

3. The 24th Division will relieve the 14th Division and 33rd Division, and will capture the objectives allotted to them.

4. The 55th Division will be in Corps reserve instead of the 24th Division.

5. Acknowledge.

S.C. Boddam-Whetham

Captain, R.A.

Brigade Major R.A. 7th Division.

Issued to :-

R.A. XV Corps	Copy No.	1	
XV Corps Heavy Artillery	,,	2	
7th Division "G"	,,	3	
14th Division "G"	,,	4	
20th Division "G"	,,	5	
24th Division "G"	,,	6	
33rd Division "G"	,,	7	
14th Divnl. Artillery	,,	8	
24th Divisional Artillery	,,	9	
33rd Divisional Artillery	,,	10	
14th Brigade R.H.A.	,,	11	(4 copies)
22nd Brigade R.F.A.	,,	12	(5 copies)
35th Brigade R.F.A.	,,	13	(5 copies)
28th Brigade R.F.A.	,,	14	(7 copies)
156th Brigade R.F.A.	,,	15	(7 copies)
Trench Mortar Officer	,,	16	
7th Divnl. Ammn. Column	,,	17	
C.R.A.	,,	18	
War Diary	,,	19 & 20	

Appendix 2

Copy No...17.......

7th DIVISIONAL ARTILLERY, OPERATION ORDER No. 28.

1. The north-east corner of DELVILLE WOOD, ALE ALLEY up to its junction with BEER TRENCH, and the NEW German trench will be attacked today.

2. Zero will be 3-10 p.m. to fit in with an attack by the XIV Corps.

3. The attack will be preceded by a heavy bombardment on the north-east portion of the WOOD, ALE ALLEY, HOP ALLEY, BEER TRENCH south of ALE ALLEY, and the NEW TRENCH. The north-east corner of DELVILLE WOOD will be cleared at 11-0 a.m. as far as an approximate line S.12.d.6.3 - S.12.d.2.0. - S.18.b.2.7 - S.18.b.5.4. - S.18.b.7.1.
The bombardment will begin at 12 noon and will include the whole of the trenches to be attacked.

4. At 2-5 p.m. the Heavy Artillery will lift off DELVILLE WOOD on to BEER TRENCH, remaining there until 2-35 p.m. After which they will lift on to PINT TRENCH, ALE ALLEY east of BEER TRENCH, and back areas.

5. Action of Divisional Artillery: Between 12 noon and 1-15 p.m. 18-prs which normally cover the area to be attacked will search and sweep within the area at a rate of 60 rounds per battery per hour. The whole of the objectives outside the WOOD to be included. 4.5" howitzers will fire on trench junctions and trenches at the same rate

1-15 p.m. to 2-0 p.m. 1 round per gun or howitzer per two minutes.

6. Batteries which will take part in the bombardment and barrages are as follows :-

"C" Group: Two 18-pr. batteries: One 4.5" how. Battery.

35th Brigade R.F.A. All batteries.

~~14th~~ 22nd Brigade R.~~F~~.A. one 18-pr. battery ~~and D/14 Battery~~.

Areas are allotted as follows :-

"C" Group: Area between ALE ALLEY(inclusive) and a line drawn parallel to and 100 yards north of ALE ALLEY.

35th Brigade R.F.A. Area between ALE ALLEY (inclusive) and a line S.18.b.9.4. - T.13.b.2.4.

One Battery 22nd Brigade R.F.A. Area between S.18.b.9.4. - T.13.b.2.4. and T.13.a.10.15 - T.13.b.4.2.

Eastern boundary of all areas: PINT TRENCH.

From 12 noon to 2-35 p.m. 14th Brigade R.H.A. will sweep the new German trench at a slow rate, lifting on to PINT TRENCH between ALE ALLEY and T.13.b.6.3. at 2-35 p.m.

7. Barrages.

Barrages:

(a) 2-0 p.m. to 2-10 p.m.

"C" Group (2 batteries) S.18.b.8.9. - S.18.b. 9. 5.

35th Brigade R.F.A. S.18.b. 9. 5. - T.13.a. 0. 2.

22nd Brigade R.F.A. (One battery) T.13.a. 0. 2. - T.13.a. 2. 0.

RATE: Two rounds per gun per minute.

(b) At 2-10 p.m. batteries will lift at the rate of 25 yards per minute until reaching BITTER TRENCH at 2-20 p.m.

"C" Group: T.13.a. 2.9. - T.13.a.20.65.

35th Brigade R.F.A. T.13.a.20.65. - T.13.a. 2. 3.

22nd Brigade R.F.A. T.13.a. 2. 3. - T.13.a. 2. 1.

RATE OF FIRE: 2-10 p.m. - 2-30 p.m. 1 round per gun per minute
2-30 p.m. - 2-35 p.m. 2 rounds per gun per minute.

(c) At 2-35 p.m. batteries will lift at the rate of 25 yards per minute until reaching a line 200 yards beyond NEW TRENCH.

"C" Group: T. 7.c. 7. 1. - T.13.a.90.85.

35th Brigade R.F.A. T.13.a.90.85. - T.13.b.25.45.

22nd Brigade R.F.A. T.13.b.25.45. - T.13.b.35.20.

RATE OF FIRE: 2-35 p.m. - 2-40 p.m. 2 rounds per gun per minute.

(d) At 2-45 p.m. 18-prs. will search forward by lifts of 25 yards per minute until arriving on the following lines :-

"C" Group: T. 7.d.35.25. - T.13.b.40.95.

35th Brigade R.F.A. T.13.b.40.95. - T.13.b.50.65.

22nd Brigade R.F.A. T.13.b.50.65. - T.13.b. 6. 3.

RATE: 1 round per gun per minute.

(e) At 3.10 p.m. All batteries will lift off PINT TRENCH on to objectives to be notified later.

8. 4.5" howitzers will from 2-0 p.m. onwards search trenches in areas allotted to their Brigades but will in no case fire less than 150 yards beyond the 18-pr barrage.

9.

9. Throughout the operation, "C" Group will cover its own defensive zone with the two 18-pr. and one 4.5" howitzer batteries not employed in the operation.

14th Brigade R.H.A. will sweep PINT TRENCH ~~with one 18-pr battery and one 4.5" howitzer battery~~.

22nd Brigade R.F.A. (less one battery) will cover the front from T.13.c.9.5. - T.13.b.6.3.

"D" Group: No change.

10. Special attention will be paid to the junction of ALE ALLEY with DELVILLE WOOD, and trench junctions in the area to be attacked.

11. O.C. 35th Brigade R.F.A. will be at the Headquarters 20th Brigade for this operation and will provide a liaison officer with the battalion carrying out the attack, - 21st Manchesters.

12. Orders for 2" trench mortars will be issued separately.

13. Orders for further operations during the afternoon may be expected by telegraph today.

14. ACKNOWLEDGE.

S. A. Boddam-Whetham.

Captain R.A.
Brigade Major R.A. 7th Division.

4th Sept. 1916.

Copies to:-

No. 1. R.A. XV Corps.
2. H.A. XV Corps.
3. 7th Division "G".
4. 20th Divn. "G".
5. 24th Divn. "G".
6. 33rd Divn. "G".
7. 55th Divn. "G".
8. 14th Divnl. Artillery.
9. 20th Divnl. Artillery.
10. 24th Divnl. Artillery.
11. 33rd Divnl. Artillery.
12. 55th Divnl. Artillery.
13. 14th Brigade R.H.A. (4 copies)

No. 14. 22nd Brigade R.F.A. (5 copies)
15. 35th Brigade R.F.A. (5 copies)
16. 28th Brigade R.F.A. (7 copies)
17. 158th Brigade R.F.A. (7 copies)
18. T.M.O. 7th Divnl. Artillery.
19. 7th Divn. Ammn. Column.
20. "X" Battery R.H.A.
21. 20th Infantry Brigade.
22. 22nd Infantry Brigade.
23. 72nd Infantry Brigade.
24. C.R.A.
25. & 26. War Diary.

Carry on to 1.45

Extend barrage Northwards to T14 A 5 3

At 1.45

1 Rd per gun per min at 1.45

at 2.45 to 2 Rds per 3 mins per gun

at 3 pm lift barrage to T 14 B 50 to T14 A 8[illegible]

[illegible] 1 Bty on Lagan Lane

guides to MONTENSCOURT at 9.30

Appendix 3

R.A. VI Corps No: S/99/5. **S E C R E T.**

CO-OPERATION OF DIVISIONAL ARTILLERY WITH R.F.C.

* *

Each Field Artillery Group of the Divisional Artillery is now provided with a wireless ground receiving station. No special individual calls are allotted to those stations except for pre-arranged shoots. The call for all stations of Divisional Artillery is the letter "Y". All Calls sent by artillery machines of No: 12 Squadron, which works with the VI Corps, are prefixed by the letter "P". In addition the pilots and observers each have a personal Call - a number. This number follows the prefix and precedes the station call, thus - P.4.Y. :-

"P" = No: 12 Squadron prefix
4 = Observer's personal Call
"Y" = Station Call (all Divnl Artillery of VI Corps).

There is a special emergency call for specially important objectives which is to be used by any machine of any Squadron in special cases as laid down in Chapter II, P.46, R.F.C. Manual. This Call is altered from time to time by G.H.Q. The call at present in force is "LL". No squadron prefix is sent and the "LL" is followed by the map sheet and map reference and short description in clear. On receipt of this call every gun that can bear on the objective is to open fire, -

e,g. LL 51B H21 c 5.6 "Infantry",

denoting: All batteries fire at infantry at H.21 c 5.6 Sheet 51B. In addition the following natures of calls may be received at a Divisional Artillery Ground Station which call for action :-

1. PY GF H21 c 5.6 followed by description in clear, guns, transport, infantry, wagons, etc. etc.

This is a call to Divisional Artillery of VI Corps to shoot at nature of target indicated at H 21 c 5.6. All guns of Divisional Artillery that can bear open rapid rate of fire and continue to shoot so long as the aeroplane observer continues to send the Call "G.F.". When the target no longer presents itself, the Observer will send down "M.Q".

"M.Q.". If no call is received from the aeroplane for three minutes batteries will cease fire.

As instructions have been received from Third Army for Test Calls to be sent frequently to Divisional Artillery the letters "G.F" will be omitted for a Test in order to enonomise ammunition.

e.g. PY H21 c 5.6

On receipt of this call all batteries that can reach the objective will fire one round per gun.

2. PY NF H21 c 5.6.

This denotes that there are guns now firing in position at H.21 c 5.6 and is a call to batteries of Divisional Artillery to engage. This call would under present conditions probably apply to an Anti-aircraft Battery in action in the open, and is to be treated as a fleeting opportunity. Fire would be continued till "M.Q." was received from the aeroplane.

3. In cases where batteries of Divisional Artillery wish to carry out a pre-arranged shoot, such a registration of cross roads, trench junctions etc., a special call is allotted to the ground station of the Group to which the battery belongs. This call would probably be a double letter call e.g "D.F"

Details of the shoot will be arranged personally between the observer and the B.C. and an intimation will be sent to the Group before the aeroplane leaves the aerodrome to carry it out. The observer on arrival will call up P4 DF "B"

P = No: 12 Squadron prefix, 4 = Observer's personal call.
DF = Special call allotted to Group for this shoot.
B = Are you receiving my signals.

The letter "K" denoting "Yes" will be put out by means of ground strips at ground station immediately this call is received.

The observer then sends P4 DF A N1

P 4 DF as before
A = stand by
N1 = Target 1.

When the battery is ready to open fire the letter "L" will be put out

APPENDIX 1

SECRET.

51st DIVISIONAL ARTILLERY

OPERATION ORDER NO.39

Reference 1/20,000 Map
MARTINPUICH.

1st August, 1916

1. Copy of Orders from Xv Corps attached.

2. The two Brigades of 33rd Divisional Artillery remaining in the line are:-
156th Brigade, R.F.A., Headquarters at S 20 a 8 4
167th Brigade, R.F.A. Headquarters at X 30 a 8 7
These Brigades less D/156 will come under the orders of the G.O.C. 51st Divisional Artillery at 4 a.m., on 2/8/16.

3. Zones are allotted as follows :-
up to 4 a.m. on 2/8/16.-
167th Brigade from S 11 b 5 0 to S 11 a 4 0
156th Brigade from S 11 a 4 0 to S 11 a 0 7
260th Brigade from S 11 a 0 7 to S 4 d 3 6
258th Brigade from S 4 d 3 6 to S 4 b 1 0
256th Brigade from S 4 b 1 0 to S 3 b 8 0
255th Brigade from S 3 b 8 0 to S 3 d 0 5

After 4 a.m., on 2/8/16.

167th Brigade from S 11 a 4 0 to S 11 a 0 7
260th Brigade from S 11 a 0 7 to S 4 d 4 5
258th Brigade from S 4 d 4 5 to S 4 b 1 0
256th Brigade from S 4 b 1 0 toS 4 a 4 0
255th Brigade from S 4 a 4 0 to S 3 b 8 0 to S 3 d 6 9
156th Brigade from S 3 d 6 9 to S 3 d 0 5

4. Acknowledge

Issued at 4 p.m. (SD) Major, R.A
Brigade Major,
51st Divisional Artillery

ack War Diary

COPY No. 19

SECRET

51st DIVISIONAL ARTILLERY
OPERATION ORDER No.41

Appendix 2

7th August,1916.

Reference 1/20,000 Map MARTINPUICH
and XV Corps Sketch Map No.X9

1. There will be two bombardments of ORCHARD TRENCH from its junction with DELVILLE WOOD to its junction with WOOD LANE /* and the Eastern point of HIGH WOOD.

/*The whole of WOOD LANE.

2. The bombardments will be from 5.30p.m., until 6.30 p.m., on 7th inst., and from 4 a.m., to 6 a.m., on 8th inst. As many field guns and howitzers as possible are to be employed.

3. The 51st Divisional Artillery will bombard WOOD LANE from S.11.a.4.0 to East corner of HIGH WOOD inclusive.

4. Zones are allotted as follows :-

18-pounder Batteries.

167th Brigade R.F.A. from S.11.a.4.0 to S.11.a.20.35
260th Brigade R.F.A. from S.11.a.20.35 to S.10.b.9.9
258th Brigade R.F.A. from S.10.b.9.9 to S.4.d.80.15
256th Brigade R.F.A. from S.4.d.80.15 to S.4.d.55.75
255th Brigade R.F.A. from S.4.d.58.68 to S.4.d.20.65
156th Brigade R.F.A. from S.4.d.18.60 to S.4.b.1.1 including the strong point.

4.5" Howr. Batteries

260th Brigade R.F.A., from S.11.a.4.0 to S.10.b.9.9
256th Brigade R.F.A., from S.10.b.9.9 to S.4.d.55.75
255th Brigade R.F.A., from S.4.d.58.68 to S.4.d.20.65 and from S.4.d.18.60 to S.4.b.1.1 including the strong point.

5. Ammunition to be fired :-

4.5" Howitzers - 60 rounds per gun } each bombardment.
18-pdrs. - 90 rounds per gun }

6. To assist XIII Corps Operations, night firing, on the usual night objectives, will be increased after midnight on the night 7th/8th August. For this, the Ammunition Allotments are doubled for the night of the 7th/8th.

7. Acknowledge by wire.

Issued at 9.45 a/m.

[signature]
Major, R.A.,
Brigade Major,
51st Divisional Artillery.

Copies Nos.	1-4	255th Brigade R.F.A.
	5-8	256th Brigade R.F.A.
	9-11	258th Brigade R.F.A.
	12-15	260th Brigade R.F.A.
	16-19	156th Brigade R.F.A.
	20-22	167th Brigade R.F.A.
	23-24	33rd Division "G"
	25	XV Corps Artillery
	26	XV Corps Heavy Artillery
	27	5th Divisional Artillery
	28	Diary
	29	Office

[illegible]
1 Copy

[illegible]

(APPENDIX 3)

OPERATION ORDER No.24
by
Brigadier-General H.S.SELIGMAN.
Commanding R.A.7th Division.

Headquarters, R.A.
23rd August 1916

1. (a) The 14th Division is to attack on the 24th August in the afternoon.

(b) Zero will be 5.45 p m.

2. Objectives are as follows :-

(a) Trench junction at T 13 c 8 5 and to establish a defensive line facing North from that point to T 13 c 4 9

(b) To take ALE ALLEY from T 13 a 5 8 to its junction with DELVILLE WOOD and to clear the wood itself.

(c) To advance and establish a line running from BEER TRENCH round DELVILLE WOOD through about S 12 central towards TEA TRENCH, and to join up with 33rd Division.

3. (a) The 33rd Division on our left will take-
(1) new trench in S 11 a and b and that part of WOOD LANE south of junction of the new trench with WOOD LANE,
(2) TEA TRENCH, and join up with 14th Division.

(b) The XlV Corps are attacking the trenches S.W. of GINCHY and also further south in conjunction with the French.

(c) The 111 Corps are also making an attack N.W. of the XV Corps front.

4. The attack will be prepared by a heavy bombardment starting two hours before zero.

5. The Infantry will be withdrawn fifty yards south and east of the junction of HOP ALLEY and BITTER TRENCH, and in the WOOD behind a line running from S 18 b 8 2 - S 12 c 00 15 - S 11 d 50 65

6. The 7th Divisional Artillery and batteries of attached Divisional Artilleries will bombard the German trenches in DELVILLE WOOD, search the ground east and north of the Wood as far as the main LONGUEVAL - FLERS Road (inclusive), and search the trench round GINCHY and the northern half of GINCHY VILLAGE.

7. ZONES and Barrages are allotted as follows :-

"C" Group. from - 2 hours to - 10 minutes.

Bombard the German trenches in DELVILLE WOOD and search the ground between INNER TRENCH and the north edge of the wood.
Left flank of zone: FLERS - LONGUEVAL Road.
Right flank of zone; point S 12 c 8 3 - S 12 d 2 4.

35th Brigade, R.F.A. - 2 hours to - 10 minutes.
Bombard German trenches in DELVILLE WOOD and search the WOOD in area in triangle - S 12 c 8 3 - S 12 d 2 4 - T 13 a 0 7.

From - 10 minutes to + 5 minutes, "C" Group and 35th Brigade, R.F.A will concentrate on INNER TRENCH and EDGE TRENCH, taking care that range is not too long.

At + 5 minutes "C" Group and 35th Brigade R.F.A. will lift forward by lifts of 25 yards every 1½ minutes, until all guns and howitzers are 200 yards behind the WOOD. Half the guns of each Brigade will then form a barrage at that range and the other half will search TEA SUPPORT TRENCH.

"C" Group from S 6 d 5 1 - T 7 a 5 3

35th Brigade R.F.A. ~~xxxxxxxxxxx~~ T 7 a 5 3 - T 7 d 2 5

At + 60 minutes all guns of "C" Group and 35th Brigade R.F.A. will concentrate on the barrage line 200 yards beyond DELVILLE WOOD and fire Shrapnel only at an intense rate.

At + 65 minutes Both Brigades will seardh forward quickly 25 yards at a time till reaching the following line:-

"C" Group S 12 a 6 4 - S 12 d 8 7

35th Brigade R.F.A. S 12 d 8 7 - T 7 c 8 2

This Barrage will continue until ~~xx~~ + 3 hour 20 minutes after which half the guns will be used to search the ground between this barrage lin e and TEA SUPPORT, the remainder forming a close barrage by sweeping.

Rate of fire. "C" Group and 35th Brigade R.F.A.

- 2 hours to + 5 minutes. 1 round per gun or howitzer per min
+ 5 minutes to + 60 minutes (1½ rounds per gun per minute,
(1 round per how. per 2 minutes)
+ 60 minutes to + 65 minutes (4 rounds per gun per minute
(1 round per how per 2 minutes
+ 65 minutes to + 75 minutes (2 rounds per gun per minute
)1 round per how per 2 minutes
+ 75 minutes to + 2 hours (1 round per gun per minute
(1 round per how per 2 minutes.

After 2 hours this rate will be halved if the situation permits, and continued until further orders.

"D" Group. (attached batteries of 33rd D.A.)

From - 2 hours to + 5 minutes search area between DELVILLE WOOD and TEA SUPPORT TRENCH.

Right boundary: ALE ALLEY

Left boundary: LONGUEVAL - FLERS Road..

From + 5 minutes to + 65 minutes same as above, but no fier to be within 500 yards of the north edge of DELVILLE WOOD.

From + 65 minutes until further orders Barrage TEA SUPPORT from T 7 d 2 5 - S 6 d 5 1.

Rate of fire.

- 2 hours to + 65 minutes (1 round per gun per minute
(1 round per how per 2 minutes.
+ 65 minutes onwards. Half the above rate

22nd Brigade R.F.A.

+ 2 hours to + 5 minutes. Search ALE ALLEY from T 13 a 0 7 to T 7 d 3 2 and BEER TRENCH from junction with ALE ALLEY to T 13 a 50 75 and the ground between ALE ALLEY and VAT ALLEY as far forward as PINT TRENCH.

At + 5 minutes to further orders 22nd Brigade will form a barrage with one battery extending from T 7 c 6 2 - T 13 a 7 9 - T 13 a 8 2.

At the same time they will continue to search the ground east of this barrage up to PINT TRENCH(inclusive) and to enfilade ALE ALLEY from T 13 a 7 9 to its junction with PINT TRENCH.

14th Brigade R.H.A.

- 2 hours to + 5 minutes Search VAT ALLEY, trench running down west edge of GINCHY from T 13 b 6 2 - T 13 c 95 50 and village of GINCHY north of a line T 13 c 9 5 - T 13 d 9 5.

at + 5 minutes to further orders 14th Brigade will form a barrage running from T 13 d 30 25 through VAT ALLEY. T 13 b 2 2 thence to T 13 b 9 2. Fire on VAT ALLEY and GINCHY TRENCH east of the barrage will continue as before

<u>Rate of fire</u> 14th Brigade R.H.A. and 22nd Brigade R.F.A.

- 2 hours to zero	1 round per gun or how per minute
zero to + 5 mins	(4 rounds per gun per minute (2 rounds per how per minute
+ 5 minutes to + 15 mins.	(2 rounds per gun per minute (1 round per howper minute
+ 15 minutes onwards	(1 round per gun per minute (½ round per how per minute

8. At 3 hours after zero howitzer fire will become intermittent and will gradually slow down, but will not cease before daylight.

18-prs will stop the close barrage but will continue to search the ground behind and all approaches and trenches within range at frequent intervals throughout the night. Batteries must be particularly on the alert for an "S.O.S" Signal.

9. Special attention will be paid by 4.5" howitzers to trench junctions and strong points in DELVILLE WOOD.

D/14 Battery R.H.A. will keep one section throughout on the area enclosed by T 13 b 2 1 - T 13 b 5 1 - T 13 d 5 3 - T 13 d 2 7.

10. S.K.Shell are allotted as follows:-

37th Battery R.F.A	150
31st Battery R.F.A.	400
35th Battery R.F.A.	250

If the wind is southerly, all the allotment of the 37th Battery and 250 of those allotted to 31st Battery will be used on the northern portion of DELVILLE WOOD up to 15 minutes before zero, after which they will be used on trench junctions further back.

If the wind is northerly, or on the case of no wind they will be used on trench junctions on the TEA SUPPORT lines up to zero and afterwards not nearer that SWITCH LINE.

The remainder of the allotment of the 31st Battery and the allotment to the 35th Battery will be used on Battalion Headquarters at T 7 d 4 0., PINT TRENCH, SWITCH TRENCH and FLERS.

11. A Section of "X" Battery R.H.A. will co-operate with enfilade fire, under special instructions given to O.C., "X" Battery.

12. H.E. or percussion shrapnel <u>only</u>, will be used in DELVILLE WOOD, in other cases two shrapnel to one H.E. will be used.

13. 2" Trench Mortars will fire under orders given by the G.O.C. 42nd Infantry Brigade.

Heavy Trench Mortars will open fire at - 2 hours and will pay special attention to T 13 a 0 7., S 18 b 60 99., S 18 b 40 99., S 12 b 2028 S 12 a 80 75., and the area 100 yards N.W. of th ~~th~~is point S 11 d 99 70.

14. As the Infantry intend to rush point T 13 a 0 7., the first ~~mf~~ jump of guns firing in this neighbourhood will be 100 yards at + 5 mins instead of lifting 25 yards at a time.

15. New O.Ps and communications must be established as soon as possible on the new front.

16. Map shewing barrage line is attached, but the co-ordinates given in these orders must be used for allotting tasks.

17. No dates or times are to be sent by telephone.

18. ACKNOWLEDGE.

(SD) Captain R.A
Brigade Major R.A. 7th Division.

WAR DIARY

Appendix

AUGUST

156th BRIGADE, R.F.A.

MONTHLY CASUALTY RETURN.

OFFICERS :

Captain C.G.Maunsell, B/156, joined 3/8/16
2nd Lt. C.E.Norton B/156, joined 1/8/16
2nd Lt. A.D.McEwen C/156, joined 2/8/16
2nd Lt. R.F.Leigh A/156, joined 2/8/16
2nd Lt. R.M.Wingfield B/156, joined 2/8/16
2nd Lt.Irvine-Watson, B/156, joined 2/8/16
Lieut. T.P.Lysaght B/156, joined 20/8/16
2nd Lt. W.J.Wreford A/156, joined 20/8/16
2nd Lt. H.E.Phipps C/156, joined 25/8/16
2nd Lt. A.W.Henley, C/156, posted from 33rd D.A.C.- 8/8/16
2nd Lt. V.Cunis, D/156, posted to 33rd D.A.C. - 8/8/16
2nd Lt.Irvine-Watson, B/156, wounded 7/8/16
2nd Lt. F.W.Price, D/156, struck off, sick 13/8/16

MEN :

Killed
2 on 5/8/16
1 on 8/8/16
1 on 9/8/16
2 on 7/8/16
1 on 11/8/16
1 on 25/8/16
1 on 30/8/16
1 on 31/8/16
10

Wounded
1 on 2/8/16
1 on 3/8/16
2 on 6/8/16
4 on 7/8/16
3 on 8/8/16
1 on 11/8/16
1 on 23/8/16
6 on 26/8/16
2 on 27/8/16
3 on 29/8/16
4 on 30/8/16
1 on 31/8/16
29

Sick Evacuated 12.

Joined 81.

Posted away 16.

HORSES :

Posted away 26.

Joined 30.

Deaths. 6.

1/9/16

[signature]
Lieut. & Adjutant,
for Lieut-Colonel,
Commanding 156th Brigade, R.F.A.

156 RFA 33 Div
Vol 8

Army Form C. 2118.

Instructions regarding War Diaries and Intelligence Summaries are contained in F. S. Regs., Part II. and the Staff Manual respectively. Title pages will be prepared in manuscript.

WAR DIARY
or
INTELLIGENCE SUMMARY.
(Erase heading not required.)

Hour, Date, Place	Summary of Events and Information	Remarks and references to Appendices
1 – 5th Sept.	Brigade in action at MONTAUBAN Operations see appendix 1. 2.	
5th.	Brigade relieved by N. Z. Artillery.	
6th.	Brigade marched to BONNAY. & were billetted there for night 6/7th.	
7th.	Brigade marched to HAVERNAS. & were billeted there for night 7/8th.	
8th.	Brigade marched to LEMEILLARD do do 8/9th	
9th.	do do to GROUCHEZ do do 9/10th	12 Sep Brigade reorganised as 6 gun batteries. The { 3 6 gun 18 pdr Batteries; 1 " 4.5 How Battery
10th	do do to HAUTEVILLE do do 10/13th	
12th	do do to WANQUETIN do do 13/14	
13th/16th.	Brigade relieved 124th Bde 37th Div Arty at ARRAS.	Wagon Lines at WANQUETIN
18th.	Brigade marched to GUADIEMPRÉ	
19th	Brigade relieved 17th Div Arty & went into action NE of SAILLY-au-BOIS.	Wagon Lines at GUADIEMPRÉ
21st.	H. Q. 156 Bde 2 sections of each 18 pdr Bty & one section of Howitzer Battery marched to WANQUETIN.	
22nd	Remainder of 156 Bde marched to WANQUETIN.	
22/23rd.	H. Q. 156 Bde & sections of Batteries as per appendix 3 came into action at ARRAS.	Wagon Lines WANQUETIN.

[signature]

(73989) W4141—463. 400,000. 9/14. H.&J.Ltd. Forms/C. 2118/10.

Instructions regarding War Diaries and Intelligence Summaries are contained in F. S. Regs., Part II. and the Staff Manual respectively. Title pages will be prepared in manuscript.

WAR DIARY
or
INTELLIGENCE SUMMARY.
(*Erase heading not required.*)

Army Form C. 2118.

Hour, Date, Place	Summary of Events and Information	Remarks and references to Appendices
22nd/30th.	Brigade in action at ARRAS, under 35th Div. Arty.	[illegible]
	[illegible]	Attached monthly casualty return.
		H. Rochfort-Boyd Lt Col Cdg 156th Bde

(73989) W4141—463. 400,000. 9/14. H.&J.Ltd. Forms/C. 2118/10.

156th BRIGADE, R.F.A.

MONTHLY CASUALTY RETURN.

Officers :- Captain W.Campbell, R.A.M.C. -- Killed -- 5/9/16
2nd Lieut. W.J.Wreford ---- Wounded - 5/9/16

Men :-	Killed	4 on 5/9/16
	Died of wounds	1 on 3/9/16
	Wounded	1 on 1st 4 on 2nd 1 on 3rd 1 on 4th 1 on 5th
	Evacuated	16
	Joined	203 (included A/167 & ½ B/167)
	Posted Away	16
Horses :-	Joined	168 (from 167th Bde)
	Posted away	59
	Deaths	1

30/9/16

[signature] 2/Lt.& Adjutant,
for Lieut-Colonel,
Commanding 156th Brigade, R.F.A.

Instructions regarding War Diaries and Intelligence Summaries are contained in F. S. Regs., Part II. and the Staff Manual respectively. Title pages will be prepared in manuscript.

WAR DIARY
or
INTELLIGENCE SUMMARY.
(*Erase heading not required.*)

156 Bde R.F.a. Vol 9

Army Form C. 2118.

Hour, Date, Place	Summary of Events and Information	Remarks and references to Appendices
Oct 4/16	Hd Qtrs 156 Bde + one section of each Battery left ARRAS + proceeded to GUADIEMPRÉ on morning of 4th.	
Oct 5th.	Hd Qtrs moved to SAILLY. one section of each Battery went into action in VII corps area.	
6th.	Remaining sections left ARRAS + proceeded to Wagon line at WANGUETAN.	
7th.	~~Night of 7th/8th~~ Remaining sections proceeded to Wagon lines at GUADIEMPRE. Night of 7/8th went into action in VII corps area.	Wire cutting was carried out daily during the month.
19th.	Night of 19/20 transferred to XIII corps. Wagon lines moved on morning of 19th to COUIN.	
22nd.	Bombardment of PUISSEUX by 18 pdrs. + heavy artillery.	Reference appendix I
26th.	a raid was carried out between the POINT + POINT 60. A, B + D Bty 156 Bde cooperated.	

H. Ruth[?] Lt. Boyd
Lt.
C.O. 156th Bde

156. BRIGADE% R.F.A.

Monthly Casualty Return.

OFFICERS:- 2/Lt. A.W.Henley ----------wounded-------30.10.16.

MEN:-

Killed.	I on 24.10.16.	
Died of wounds.	NIL	
Wounded.	I on 9.10.16.	
	2 on 19.10.16.	
	I on 20.10.16.	
	3 on 24.10.16.	
	I on 25.10.16.	
Evacuated.	29.	
Joined.	39.	
Posted away.	29.	

HORSES:-

Joined.	45.
Posted away.	20.
Deaths.	NIL.

31.10.16.

E.F.[illegible]
Lt. & Adjt.
for O.C.
156. Brigade. R.F.A.

APPENDIX 1

33rd D.A. No.BM/S/835

Concentrations on villages will take place on 22nd instant :-

PUSIEUX,	3.30 p.m. to 3.50	) Guns and howitzers that can bear
SERRE.	4 p.m. to 4.20 p.m.	) on these places will be required-

----

Instructions regarding War Diaries and Intelligence Summaries are contained in F. S. Regs., Part II. and the Staff Manual respectively. Title Pages will be prepared in manuscript.

WAR DIARY
or
~~INTELLIGENCE SUMMARY~~

(Erase heading not required.)

Army Form C. 2118.

156 Bde R.F.A.
Vol 10

Place	Date	Hour	Summary of Events and Information	Remarks and references to Appendices
	Nov. 2nd 1916.		Night of 2/3, the 156 Brigade co-operated in a raid just north of THE POINT.	Wire-cutting was carried out daily until the 12th instant
	Nov. 11th 1916	3pm	Made responsible for the artillery support of the 31st Division front.	
	Nov. 13th 1916	5am	Attack on SERRE. Covered infantry advance with creeping barrage + maintained barrage on support & communication trenches throughout the day.	
	Nov. 14th 1916		Relieved of responsibility of the defence of the front. C/156 + D/156 withdrew to wagon lines at COIN, on night 14/15.	
	Nov. 15th 1916		Night of 15/16 A/156 + B/156 withdrew to wagon lines at COIN.	
	Nov 16th 1916		156 Brigade H.Qs. withdrew to LOUVENCOURT	
	Nov. 22nd 1916		156 Brigade marched to VILLERS BOCAGE	
	Nov. 23rd 1916		156 Brigade marched to AIRAINES	

[illegible] [illegible]
Commanding 156th Brigade R.F.A.

2449 Wt. W14957/M90 750,000 1/16 J.B.C. & A. Forms/C.2118/12.

drew off, having apparently, by sheer superiority of marksmanship, inflicted some thirty or forty casualties at the cost of a single officer wounded. A troop of the 16th Lancers, which had been sent to their support, gave chase to a hostile patrol on the way, and came suddenly upon a party of Jäger on the hill immediately to west of Péronnes. The troops rode straight over the Jäger, charged through them again on the return journey, and then left them to "E" Battery R.H.A., which had unlimbered to cover its return. Altogether, the cavalry was heartened by its work on this day, being satisfied that it was superior to the German horsemen, both mounted and dismounted, both with rifle and with sword.

The cumulative effect on the British cavalry commanders of the encounters during the day was the conviction that German infantry in great force was in close support of the German cavalry.[x] They had made reports in that sense on the previous day, and they were now more than ever confirmed in their opinion. Aerial reconnaissance during the forenoon did not tend to shake this view. One flying party landing at Beaumont (about twelve miles east of Maubeuge) to take in petrol, learned from General de Mas-Latrie, the commander of the French XVIII. Corps, that General Sordet had on the 21st encountered German infantry north of the Sambre Canal, and had been compelled to fall back. This accounted for his movement westward to Binche.

x It should be borne in mind that a German Cavalry Division is a force of all arms (see Appendix 4), containing not only cavalry and horse artillery, but several battalions of Jäger, each with its machine gun company, and a machine gun Abtheilung. It is now known that other infantry battalions were attached, e.g., an ordinary Bavarian infantry battalion was with the 3rd Cavalry Division, in addition to its Jäger (vide Hauptmann Rutz's Bayernkämpfe).

Please supply the following documents:-

	Remarks

Date ____________ Signature: ____________

SECRET. Copy No. 4.

166 Brigade Order No.3.

Ref.

Map , HEBUTERNE Sheet 57d N.E. Ed. 3a.

Nov. 6th 1916.

1. Raids will be carried out by the 13th and 14th Btns. Y & L Regt. on the night of 6/7th inst, the 31st Div. Arty will cut wire at points of entry.
   14th Y. & L. will enter at points K.17 a.95.60 and K.17 b.00.45.
   13th Y. & L. at K.17 d.12.12.

2. Time of entering as of raids, and will be at 1 a.m. on 7th inst.
   If successful, raiding parties will remain in German trenches one hour.

3. First Bombardment. From zero minus one hour fifty minutes to zero minus one hour thirty minutes, 33rd Div. Arty., Heavy Artillery and 31st Div. Arty will join in heavy bombardment of enemy front and support lines.
   The 33rd Div. Arty. from K.17 d.2.6. to K.23 b.4.6.

4. Second Bombardment. At zero minus two minutes an intense bombardment will be opened on the enemy support lines.
   The 33rd Div. Arty on the same front.
   4.5" Hows 166th Brigade R.F.A. on third line.

   At zero plus two minutes guns on support line, 166th Brigade will lift to barrages as shewn in tables, to enable the infantry to advance to support line.
   The artillery bombardment will be intense for twenty minutes then steady for twenty minutes when it will gradually die away.

5. Directly the second bombardment opens at zero minus two minutes, the Infantry will pass through the ~~gap~~ wire and enter enemy trench at, or if possible, before Zero.
   At zero the Infantry will push on as fast as possible to enemy second line. If little opposition is met with, the parties will push on further until the enemy is encountered.

6. Visual Signalling stations will be manned.

7. Time will be synchronised separately from Brigade H.Q. about 5 p.m.

8. Acknowledge.

War diary

E. M. [signature]

Lieut. R.F.A.
Adjutant. 166th Brigade R.F.A.

Copy No.1 to A/166.
,, 2 ,, B/166.
,, 3 ,, D/166.
,, 4 file.

Army Form C. 2118. 3

WAR DIARY
or
INTELLIGENCE SUMMARY

(Erase heading not required.)

Instructions regarding War Diaries and Intelligence Summaries are contained in F. S. Regs., Part II. and the Staff Manual respectively. Title Pages will be prepared in manuscript.

156 Bde R F A

Vol XI

Place	Date	Hour	Summary of Events and Information	Remarks and references to Appendices
	Dec 1-5th		Brigade in [illegible] AIRAINES	
	5-15th		Relieved 127th Division French	
	25th		Assisted in Fourth Army artillery attack	
	31.		Relieved by 166 Bde RFA + marched to No 6 AREA	

A H [illegible] Lt Col
Comdg 156 Bde RFA

JANUARY. 1917

Instructions regarding War Diaries and Intelligence Summaries are contained in F. S. Regs., Part II. and the Staff Manual respectively. Title Pages will be prepared in manuscript.

WAR DIARY
or
INTELLIGENCE SUMMARY
(Erase heading not required.)

156th Brigade. R.F.A.

Vol 12

Army Form C. 2118

Place	Date	Hour	Summary of Events and Information	Remarks and references to Appendices
N. of MAUREPAS	5th		H.Q. 166th Brigade R.F.A. changed over to 156th Brigade R.F.A., & H.Q. 156th Brigade became H.Q. 166th Brigade. R.F.A.	
			Lt Col C.G. STEWART C.M.G. D.S.O., Commanding 156th Brigade. R.F.A.	
			Lt. Col. A.H. BRIDGES, Commanding 166 Brigade. R.F.A.	
"	10th		Capt J.R. McCALLUM transferred from B to D/166. Lt S.M. WOOD to B/166.	
			Lt H.M. STANFORD. M.C, B/166 appointed Adjutant, 156th Brigade R.F.A., vice Lt. S.M. WOOD. to B/166.	
"	12th		Withdrew from action N. of MAUREPAS. & proceeded to Wagon Lines at Camp 21 SUZANNE.	
Camp 14.	13th		Proceeded to Camp 14. 166th Brigade re-organized. A/166 became A/26. B/166 became C/93. 1 Section D/166 to D/156 & 1 Section to D/162.	
"	14th		Major H.A.T. BARSTOW. from D/166 to D/156. Capt. J.R. McCALLUM from D/166 to 162nd Bde.	
			2/Lt. A.H. WHITING from D/166 to 162nd Bde. 2/Lt J.T. GORMAN & 2/Lt T.Q. HARVEY from D/166 to D/156.	
"	20th		Batteries 156th Brigade joined Brigade H.Q. at Camp 14.	
VAUX WOOD	21st		Left Camp 14 & proceeded to wagon line at VAUX WOOD.	
W. of CLERY	22nd		Batteries relieved French & went into action W. of CLERY.	
			Lt. Col. C.G. STEWART C.M.G. D.S.O, Commanding Left Group - 33rd Divl. Arty.	

H.M. Stanford Lt R.F.A.
for Lt. Col.
COMMANDING 156TH BRIGADE. R.F.A.

1875 Wt. W593/826 1,000,000 4/15 J.B.C. & A. A.D.S.S./Forms/C. 2118.

SECRET.

"V"

PRELIMINARY BOMBARDMENT
April 4th and night April 4/5th 1917.

Unit	Task.	Time.	Ammn:	Remarks.
A/156	Enfilade HUNTINGDON Trench	7 a.m to 7 p.m.	420 rounds. 50% AX Blue Nose. 50% A.	15 rds an hour at G.24 b.5.5. 5 rds an hour on H.19 a.1½.8.(same line as above) 15 rds an hour H.19 a.3.9 & 3½.9½
	Ditto.	7 p.m to 7 a.m.	Not less than 432 rds AX Blue Nose.	6 Battery salvoes an hour at irregular intervals at HUNTINGDON Trench G.24 b.4.8 to H.19 b.4.8½.
B/156	Enfilade HUNTINGDON Trench	7 a.m to 7 p.m.	250 rds. 50% AX Blue Nose. 50% T.S.	10 rds an hour H.19 a.3.9 & 3½.9½ 15 rds an hour H.19 a.9.8. and H.19 b.0.8.
	Wire Cutting E.B.		75 rds T.S. at least 40% on graze 75 rds A.X Non-delay.	Increasing wire gap at E.B.
	Keeping gap at E.B. open	7 p.m. to 7 a.m.	40 rds T.S. effective corrector. 40 rds HE Blue Nose	Total 80 rds to stop work.
	Search Area H.19 b.		Not less than 350 rds. H.E. with delay. 25% T.S. 75% HE Blue Nose.	6 battery salvoes (5 or 6 guns) an hour at likely man killing spots in Area H.19 b. but A/156 is shelling HUNTINGDON Trench as far East as H.19 b.4.8½.
C/156	Wire Cutting F.A and F.B.	7 a.m to 7 p.m.	80 rds T.S. at least 40% on graze. 80 rds H.E. non-delay.	Increasing gap at F.B.
			80 rds T.S. 80 rds H.E. Non-delay	Increasing gaps at F.A. Support line & GLOUCESTER TERRACE.
	Enfilade HUNTINGDON TRENCH		120 rds. 25% AX Blue Nose 25% AX Non-delay 50% T.S.	10 rds an hour on H.19 b.1½.8 to 4.8.
	Keep gaps at F.A and F.B. open.	7 p.m to 7 a.m.	40 rds T.S. effective corrector 40 rds HE with delay	Total 80 rds during the night to stop work at F.A.
			Ditto.	Ditto on F.B.
			Not less than 276 rds AX Blue Nose.	6 salvoes of 4 guns each hour into FRED'S WOOD

13. The Brigade will take over defence of a portion of the line on morning of 4th, from that hour the Brigade will have to keep up a liaison officer with staff, and at night will have to man the Brigade O.P. with one officer three N.C.Os and telephone staff.

14. <u>Miscellaneous</u>.
(a) Each battery will carry strapped on wagon bodies two half bridges. They are not intended for this battle. Time and place of drawing them will be notified.
(b) 32nd D.A. have asked for one water barrel, a lot of petrol tins, three pack saddles per battery.
(c) All G.S. wagons go to the train on "Y" day and batteries will have to be independent of them thenceforward.
(d) All occupied cellars and dugouts must be provided with air tubes and a pick and shovel must be kept in each. If possible adjacent cellars and dugouts should be connected by an underground passage.

15. Orders will be issued about the following as soon as fresh orders, which are expected, are received:-
(a) Position of wagon lines and time of occupying them.
(b) Water.
(c) Route and time of move to second position.
✓(d) Bombardment.
✓(e) Barrages.
Orders will be issued later about:-
(a) Rations.
(b) Ammunition.
(c) Reports.
✓(d) Communications.
✓(e) O.Ps.
✓(f) Liaison.
✓(g) S.O.S.s.
✓(h) Use of Very pistols.
✓(i) Medical.
✓(j) Barrages.
✓(k) Testing box respirators.

April 2nd 1917.

Captain R.F.A.
Adjutant 158th Brigade R.F.A.

Unit.	Task.	Time.	Ammn:	Remarks.
D/156.	No firing - they will be continuously firing on Y/Z night.			

NOTES:-

1. In map shooting at an enfilade trench the amount of sweep to be ordered depends on the accuracy of registration and knowledge of atmospheric conditions; if these are pretty well known, sweep 15 minutes gives good results.
2. Guns must not be fired when deficient of oil. If shortage of oil makes such a course necessary, oil must be taken from one gun to fill up the other five.

April 3rd 1917.

[signature] Capt. R.F.A.
Adjutant, 156th Brigade R.F.A.

W

SECRET.

PROGRAMME OF FIRING DAY AND NIGHT - 156th BRIGADE R.F.A.
W DAY.

Unit.	Time.	Task.	Ammn:	Remarks.
A/156	7 a.m to 7 p.m.	Nil.	Nil.	
	7 p.m to 7 a.m.	As on night of V/W.		
B/156	7 a.m to 7 p.m.	Wire at:- 1. GOSFORD TERRACE 2. E.B.	(100 AX Non-delay (100 A. Perc: 60 A or AX.	To enlarge gaps.
	7 p.m to 7 a.m.	As on night of V/W.		Gap in GOSFORD TERRACE must be kept open out of same allotment of ammunition.
C/156	7 a.m to 7 p.m.	Wire at:- 1. F.A. Support Line 2. F.A. GLOUCESTER TERRACE 3. F18.	60 A. Perc: (100 A. Perc: (100 AX Non-delay 100 A or AX	To enlarge gaps.
	7 p.m to 7 a.m.	As on night V/W.		
D/156	7 a.m to 7 p.m.	Bombard HALF Trench in Brigade Zone. SUPPORT LINES in Brigade Zone. Enfilade HUNTINGDON Trench.	100 rds per Howitzer.	Rate of fire not to exceed 3 rds per Bty per min: unless to take advantage of fleeting targets.
	7 a.m to 7 p.m.	Bombard:- G.24 d.40.76 (T.M) G.24 d.40.78 (T.M) G.24 b.62.00 (Telephone exchange.) Southern half of FRED'S WOOD. H.19 b.40.66 H.19 b.40.85 Work at [illegible]. H.20 a.34.10 Southern face of FEUCHY WOLK	 72 rounds 72 ,, 72 ,, 120 ,, 72 ,, 72 ,, 120 ,, 120 ,,	AX Blue Nose should be used with 1st 2nd & 3rd charges at trenches. Either Blue Nose or non-delay at emplacements etc.
	7 p.m to	G.24 d.2.9. G.24 d.20.97 G.24 b.05.26. G.24 a.83.23. H.19 b.40.66. H.19 b.40.85.	72 rds per Howitzer.	3 salvoes per hour at irregular intervals.

S E C R E T.

Programme of Firing for X Day and X/Y night.

Unit.	Time.	Task	Ammn:	Remarks.
A/156	7 a.m to 7 p.m.	As for W Day	Not less than 72 rds per gun to be fired during 12 hrs darkness, in salvoes.	H.E. blue nose will be used. Non-delay fuzes will be reserved for use on communications and on bombarded areas.
	7 p.m to 7 a.m.	Search Southern Third of Bde Zone in G.24 & ~~[illegible]~~. the whole of square H.19		
-B/156	7 a.m to 7 p.m.	As for W Day.	Not less than 6 salvoes per hour at irregular intervals.	
	7 p.m to 7 a.m.	Search Central Third of Bde Zone in G.24 & ~~[illegible]~~. the whole of square H.19. Gaps in wire.		
C/156	7 a.m to 7 p.m.	As for W Day.		
	7 p.m to 7 a.m.	Search Northern third of Bde Zone in G.24 & ~~[illegible]~~ + the whole of square H.19 Gaps in wire.		
D/156.	7 a.m to 7 p.m.	As for W Day.		
	7 p.m to 7 a.m.	As for night of W/X.		

NOTE:- Brigade Zone for purposes of bombardment is:-

RIGHT Boundary G.24 d.00.78 - H.19 b.00.15 - H.20 a.30.00, thence along Southern edge of Railway.

LEFT Boundary G.24 a.66.20 - 78.27 - to Northern end of FRED'S WOOD -

H.19 b.00.77 - 47.75, thence Eastwards, halfway between Railway and river.

April 5th. 1917.

Capt. R.F.A.
Adjutant, 156th Brigade R.F.A.

S E C R E T.

PROGRAMME OF FIRING FOR "Y" DAY.

Unit.	Time.	Task.	Ammunition.	Remarks.
A/156	Z -24hrs. to Z -22 hrs.	Bombard southern third of first system of trenches in Bde zone.	60rds per gun	Arrangements must be made to check the corrector at the hour of zero on Y day, due attention being paid to the effect of low temperature in the event of zero being at an early hour.
	Z -22hrs. to Z -20hrs.	Bombard southern third of second system of trenches.	60rds per gun	
	Z -15hrs ~~to Zero.~~	As for night X/Y	72rds per gun	
B/156	Z -24hrs. to Z -22hrs.	Bombard central third of first system of trenches in Bde zone.	60rds per gun	
	Z -22hrs to Z -20hrs.	Bombard central third of second system of trenches.	60rds per gun	
	Z -18hrs to Z -15hrs.	Wirecutting at E.B.	90rds per gun	
	Z -15hrs to Zero	As for night X/Y	72rds per gun	
C/156	Z -24hrs to Z -22hrs.	Bombard northern third of first system of trenches in Bde zone.	60rds per gun	
	Z -20hrs to Z -18hrs.	Wirecutting at F.A.		
	Z -22hrs to Z -20hrs.	Bombard northern third of second system of trenches.	60rds pergun	
	Z -18hrs to Z -20hrs.	Wirecutti g at E.B.	90rds per gun	
	Z -15hrs to Zero.	As for night X/Y	72rds per gun	
D/156	Z -24 hrs to Z -22hrs.	Bombard first system of trenches.	60rds per How.	
	Z -22hrs to Z -20hrs.	Bombard. second system.	60rds per How	
	Z -20hrs to Z -18hrs.	Bombard first system.	60rds per How	
	Z -18hrs to Z -15hrs.	Bombard second system.	90rds per How	
	Z -15hrs to Z -11hrs.	HUNTINGDON Tr. H.19 b.40.20 to H.19 a.30.90	60rds per How	
		H.19 b.40.60	10rds per How	
		H.20 a.55.10.	50rds per How	
	Z -15hrs to Zero.	See special orders.		

7.3.1917

S E C R E T.

Lethal and Lachrymatory Shell Bombardment by D/156.
~~Z~~- "Y" Day.

Targets:- (i) H.26 b.98.95) Nr Pit These co-ordinates are the
(ii) H.22 c.10.84) centres of two batteries.

Time.	Target.	Ammunition.	Rate of fire.
Zero - 10 hrs.	(i)	100 Lethal, from whole battery.	Maximum.
then switch onto	(ii)	100 Lethal.	Maximum.
Remainder of period Zero -10 hrs to Zero -4hrs.	(i) and (ii)	525 Lachrymatory	Deliberate.
Zero -4hrs to Zero -3 hrs.	Nil	Nil	Nil.
Zero - 3 hrs	(i)	100 Lethal	Maximum.
then switch whole battery onto	(ii)	100 Lethal	Maximum.
Remainder of period Zero -3 hrs to Zero -2 hrs.	(i) and (ii)	175 Lachrymatory.	
Zero -2hrs to Zero -1hr.15mins.	Nil	Nil	Nil.
Zero -1hr. 15.mins.	(i)	100 Lethal.	Maximum.
then	(ii)	100 Lethal	Maximum.
Remainder of period Zero -1 hr. 15 mins to Zero -15 mins.	(i) and (ii)	165 Lethal.	

Total of expenditure:- 765 Lethal.
700 Lachrymatory.

For above shoot shell will be classified thus:-

Lachrymatory S.K. or P.S.
Lethal O.B.R or J or J.B.R.

If the conditions are so unsuitable as to render Chemical Shell useless, Batteries must be prepared to carry on the work with ordinary shell, but these would have to come out of the next day's allotment.

As there is likely to be some chemical shell left behind in the position when the battery advances, boards must be prepared now, painted "Dangerous chemical shell", to put on each dump when leaving.

April 5th. 1917.

Capt. R.F.A.
Adjutant, 156th Brigade R.F.A.

FEBRUARY 1917

Instructions regarding War Diaries and Intelligence Summaries are contained in F. S. Regs., Part II. and the Staff Manual respectively. Title Pages will be prepared in manuscript.

WAR DIARY
or
INTELLIGENCE SUMMARY
(Erase heading not required.)

156th Brigade R.F.A.

Army Form C. 2118

Vol 13

Place	Date	Hour	Summary of Events and Information	Remarks and references to Appendices
P.C. OUVRAGE	5th		Major. T. E. DURIE. M.C., posted to A/156 from H.Q. 33rd Div. Arty.	
"	7th	11 pm.	Assisted 100th Infantry Brigade during raid on enemy's trenches where joining the BETHUNE Rd. Party of Infantry & Engineers entered German lines & remained there 25 minutes. 1 machine gun & 2 prisoners were brought back, & 10 Germans were killed in the trenches. 2 dug-outs full of Germans were blown in. Casualties to raiding party small, & apparently caused by enemy shell fire. (Copy of letter from G.O.C., 100th Infantry Bde re wire cutting attached.)	
"	25th		Lt-Col. NEVINSON, 33rd Brigade. R.F.A, took over command of Left Group R.A, 33rd Div.	
"	26th		Lt-Col. C.G. STEWART, C.M.G., D.S.O., proceeded on leave.	
"	27th/28th		Batteries assisted Infantry during raids on enemy's trenches at PEKLY BULGE. at 8.40 pm & 1. a.m. (Copy of report on raids attached).	

[illegible]
for Lt Col
COMMANDING 156TH BRIGADE, R.F.A.

Headquarters,
100th Infantry Brigade.

9th February,1917.

Officer Commanding,
156th Brigade R.F.A.

I should be glad if you would convey to the batteries under your command including those of the 14th Brigade the appreciation of the 9th H.L.I. of the great assistance rendered by them in preparing for and carrying out the recent raid.

My own appreciation has been expressed in the following extract of the report which I have furnished to G.O.C., 33rd Division.

"The preliminary cutting of the wire
"by the artillery was most carefully and
"effectively carried out, especially consider-
"ing the very short time available for the
"purpose.
"The arrangements for this and for the
"artillery barrage during the raid were made
"by Lieut-Colonel C.G.STEWART, C.M.G., D.S.O.,
"Commanding 156th Brigade Royal Field
"Artillery and could not have been better.
"Preliminary bombardment of the actual
"portion of the line to be entered, whilst
"the raiding party was getting out and forming
"up in "No Man's Land" was entirely confined
"to Stokes gun, Lewis gun and Rifle Grenade fire
"no lifts or changing of direction were there-
"fore entailed in the Artillery arrangements,
"this considerably simplified their task".

Sd W.BAIRD. Brigadier General,
Commanding 100th Infantry Brigade

33rd Division. CONFIDENTIAL

Summary of Intelligence - 28th Feb. 1917.

1. OPERATIONS

(a) CLERY SECTOR. Last night at 8.40 p.m. and 1 a.m. raiding parties entered the enemy's lines at PEKLY BULGE. The first party, who remained in enemy's front line for half an hour, captured 1 wounded and 6 unwounded Germans and killed 6. The second party occupied the enemy's line for 65 minutes, penetrating into his second line (PEKLY WALK) and bringing back 15 prisoners: in addition, 30 of the enemy are known to have been killed and 6 dug-outs were bombed.

The prisoners belonged to the Kaiser Franz Regt. and Alexander Regt., forming part of the 2nd Guards Division. This Division has relieved the 29th Division in the line.

Our artillery barrage was very good during both raids.

Our Stokes Mortars fired 1400 rounds in conjunction with these operations.

The enemy is firing a considerable number of Very lights from his support line now.

Patrols report that no sound of occupation was heard in HERSFELD TRENCH last night, but in the neighbourhood of the BETHUNE ROAD the enemy was observed to be standing about and the sound of driving stakes and of digging out mud was heard.

The sap leading from enemy's trench to the crater on the Road appears to be laid with trench-boards.

3. ARTILLERY.

(a) Last night, 27/28th Feb., our artillery supported the raid carried out by us on PEKLY BULGE. We bombarded HERSFELD TRENCH at the same time to simulate an attack and divert attention.

Medium T.M. Batts. also fired in connection with the raid

Wire-cutting was started today at I.13.a.05.20. with satisfactory results as far as could be seen. A lot of wire is lying about here and is badly knocked about, but it is difficult to say whether a gap has been cut right through.

33

Army Form C. 2118

MARCH – 1917

WAR DIARY
or
INTELLIGENCE SUMMARY
(Erase heading not required.)

156 Bde RFA

Instructions regarding War Diaries and Intelligence Summaries are contained in F. S. Regs., Part II. and the Staff Manual respectively. Title Pages will be prepared in manuscript.

Vol 14

Place	Date	Hour	Summary of Events and Information	Remarks and references to Appendices
	10th/11		Half batteries withdrew from action and marched to wagon lines at VAUX WOOD. H.Q. of 156th Bde. taken over by H.Q. 181 Bde. 40 Division.	
	11.	8AM	Half batteries marched to VAUX-SUR-SOMME.	
	11/12		Half batteries withdrew from action and marched to wagon lines at VAUX-WOOD	
VAUX-SUR-SOMME	12.	8AM	Half batteries and Bde. H.Q. marched to VAUX-SUR-SOMME.	
	6.		Lt H.M. Stanford, Adjutant, 156th Brigade, posted to 33rd Brigade, 8th Division	
	6		2/Lt F.L. LEE, 33rd Brigade, 8th Division, posted to 156th Brigade, and appointed Adjutant Vice Lt H.M. Stanford	
	10.		2/Lt N. GRANT, from the Base to this Brigade and ~~posted~~ attached to B/156	
	12		2/Lt E H PRIOR, R.F.A. 166th Brigade, posted to C/156	
	20.		Lt Col G G STEWART, C.M.G., D.S.O., appointed Brigadier General and placed in command of 33rd Div. Arty. with effect from 20/3/17	
	25		The Bde. marched from VAUX-SUR-SOMME to TALMAS.	
	27.		The Bde. marched to BEALCOURT	
	28.		The Bde. marched to REBREUVE.	
	29.		The Bde. marched to DUISANS. Bde. H.Q. marched to ARRAS and ~~[illegible]~~ billeted at 6 Rue Jeanne d'Arc.	
	30.		Lt Col B Butler, R.F.A. took over command of this Brigade.	
			The personnel of batteries went into billets in Arras.	
			A. B. /156 put guns in wire cutting positions at G 22 d 75 55 and G 22 d 55 55.	
	30		Capt Lutyens and Capt. Pringle attached to 162nd Bde R.F.A	
			2/Lt E.H. PRIOR and 2/Lt F.L. LEE appointed a/Captains	
	31		Major T.E. DURIE, M.C. appointed Brigade major 33rd Div. Arty. with effect from 20/3/17.	

F.L. Lee Capt R.F.A.
Adjutant 156 Bde. R.F.A

1875 Wt. W593/826 1,000,000 4/15 J.B.C. & A. A.D.S.S./Forms/C. 2118.

"A" - No 6

S E C R E T.

31st March 1917.

LEFT SUB GROUP ORDER No. 2.

Reference 15th Divisional Artillery Preliminary Instructions.

No. 1.

Para. 1, sub-para (II). Brigades will render a progress report to this Office at 6.0.p.m. daily till work is completed.

Sub-para (IV). Batteries will occupy their positions before dawn on 3.4.17. Registration will be completed on 3.4.17. A report will be rendered with the progress of work report daily showing (1) Number of guns in action in each position (2) State of registration.

Sub-para (V). Expense dumps for 200 rounds should be made at each gun. The filling of these dumps will afford an opportunity of checking the ammunition for defective fuzes and rounds.

Para. 2, sub-para (I). The map location of any supplementary O.Ps. chosen is to be reported to this office.

Sub-para (III). These diagrams must be submitted at once.

Para. 3, sub-para (I). The mobile equipment of units of the 33rd Divisional Artillery is to be complete at the conclusion of these operations.

Para. 4, sub-para (IV). Wagon lines will be arranged by Brigade Commanders. Map locations of places chosen to be reported to this office as soon as possible.

Sub-para (V). Steel girders have been asked for. These will be carried under the body of the ammunition wagon. The teams will have to be unhooked and led over the trench and the vehicles run over by hand.

Para. 8. Barrels will be supplied in lieu of tanks. Indents should be submitted at once for any petrol tins required.

Para. 9. These springs will not be available. Any guns requiring new springs must be sent to the I.O.M. who will establish a forward workshop at No. 4, RUE DE LILLE, G.21.d.4.9.

No. 2.

Para. 2. Times of advance of Batteries will be notified later.

Para. 3, sub-para (II) (b). All Batteries of the 33rd Divisional Artillery will advance by the following route :-

Battery position - G.22.a.70.50 - G.22.d.50.88 - G.23.c. 2.8. - Forward position.

No. 3.

Para 3. Liaison Officers will be detailed as follows :-

With 45th Infantry Brigade, A/Capt.E.H.PRIOR, 156th Bde. R.F.A.

With Right Battalion. A Subaltern to be detailed by O.C. 156th Brigade, R.F.A.

With Left Battalion. A Subaltern to be detailed by O.C. 162nd Brigade, R.F.A.

P.T.O

(No. 3. Para.3. continued) One F.O.O. from each Brigade will be detailed as Sub-group F.O.Os. They will occupy LYDD O.P. (No.74) and will be in communication with Sub-group H.Q. They will observe the situation for the Sub-group and the fire of their own Brigades if required. They will remain at the O.P. till the BROWN LINE is captured and consolidated. Rations and blankets should be taken.

Communications from this O.P. to Sub-group H.Q. will be maintained by the Signal Officer 33rd Divisional Artillery.

O.C. 162nd Brigade, R.F.A. will detail the officer responsible for carrying the Sub-group communications forward and each Brigade will detail six telephonists.

Names of officers and telephonists detailed are to be submitted to this office as soon as possible.

No. 4.

Para. 1. The preliminary bombardment will commence about 96 hours before Zero.

The dividing line between 156th and 162nd Brigades for the bombardment will be the line G.24.a.65.20 - G.24.a.84.25 - G.24.b.37.38 - N.W. corner of FREDS WOOD - H.19.b.00.74 and thence a line midway between the River SCARPE and the ARRAS - DOUAI Railway. Any points on this line are included in 156th Brigade Zone. 156th Brigade will have the Southern and 162nd Brigade the Northern Zone.

Wire-cutting. Gaps will be cut as follows :-

156th Brigade, R.F.A.

Gap FA in wire of SUPPORT LINE and GLOUCESTER TERRACE about G.24.b.2.1 and G.24 b.37.13.
Gap EB in wire of HALF TRENCH about H.19.a.60.25.
Gap FB in wire of HALF TRENCH about H.19.a.55.45.

162nd Brigade, R.F.A.

Gap IA in wire of SUPPORT LINE and GLOUCESTER TERRACE about G.24.b.15.20 and G.24.b.40.30.
Gap GA in wire of HALF TRENCH about H.19.a.50.60.
Gap HA in wire of HALF TRENCH about H.19.a.40.75.

Para. 5. RATIONS. This paragraph applies to units of the 15th Divisional Artillery. Substitute the following :-

RATIONS. At 11.0.p.m. on Z day units of the 33rd Divisional Artillery will be in possession of the following rations :-

Men. 3 Iron Rations for consumption on Z+1, Z+2 and Z+3 days.
1 Emergency Ration per man.

Horses. Oats for Z+1, Z+2 and Z+3.

Indents for these rations should be submitted to the Staff Captain, 33rd Divisional Artillery at once. It should also be stated how many units wish to draw in ARRAS and how many in the wagon line.

T. Elsworthe [signature]

Major, R.A.

Brigade Major, 33rd Divisional Artillery.

APRIL 1917

Instructions regarding War Diaries and Intelligence Summaries are contained in F. S. Regs., Part II. and the Staff Manual respectively. Title pages will be prepared in manuscript.

WAR DIARY
or
INTELLIGENCE SUMMARY.
(Erase heading not required.)

156th Brigade R.F.A.

Army Form C. 2118.

33rd

Vol 15

Place	Date	Hour	Summary of Events and Information	Remarks and references to Appendices
ARRAS	4th		Major H. McA. RICHARDS joined & posted to command A/156	
"	9th 10th 11th		Assisted 15th Div. in general attack on German 1st & 3rd lines. (Copy of orders attached).	"A"
"	12th		Left ARRAS & proceeded to forward H.Q. at FEUCHY.	
FEUCHY	13th		Lieut. L.M. BLOMENSTOK admitted to hospital & subsequently invalided to England	
"	14th		2/Lieut. F.W. PRICE & 2/Lieut. B. SALL joined & posted to D & B Batteries respectively.	
"	19th		2/Lieut (Temp. Captain) C.R. BURRIDGE attached.	
"	23rd		Assisted 17th Div. (in conjunction with 29th & 15th Divisions on Right & 51st Division on left) in general attack. (~~Copy of orders attached~~)	"B"
"	25th		Capt. E.G. LUTYENS C/156 & Capt. W.G. PRINGLE D/156 posted to D & C/162 respectively. Lieut. F.L. LEE transferred to D/156 from Bde. H.Q., 2/Lieut. B.L. OXLEY D/156 appointed Adjutant 156th Bde. vice Lieut. F.L. LEE. 2/Lieut. D STUART A/156 to Bde. H.Q. as Orderly Officer, vice Lieut. L.M. BLOMENSTOK, to England.	
"	28th		Assisted 12th Division (in conjunction with 3rd Div on Right, & 34th Divn on left) in general attack. (~~Copy of orders attached~~)	"C"
			Total Casualties during month:-	
			Officers:- NIL.	
			Other Ranks:- Killed in action 11.	
			Wounded 34.	
			[illegible] Lt.-Col. Commanding 156th Brigade. R.F.A.	

2353 Wt. W2544/1454 700,000 5/15 D. D. & L. A.D.S.S./Forms/C. 2118.

136th BRIGADE INSTRUCTIONS No.1.

April 2nd 1917

1. The following summary of orders received to date supersedes 15th Div. Preliminary Instructions Nos.1 - 7, also Left sub-group Order Nos.1 - 2. Any of these in possession of batteries are therefore now to be destroyed.

2. SCHEME. In the attack on Z day, the 15th Div have been alloted three objectives; these objectives are:-

First... BLACK Line H.28 a.3.8. through FRED'S WOOD to the River.
Second.. BLUE Line H.26 a.3.6. - H.20 a.3.9. - H.13 d.8.3.
Third... BROWN Line. The enemy defences in H.28 and northwards to the River.
also the high ground in H.29 c and a, i.e., the W. slopes of ORANGE HILL.
(Note) After the capture of the BROWN Line the 46th Infantry Bde will push forward patrols to secure this.

R. Left Sub Group

156 Bde / R. Bn

3. The 15th Div will attack with two Brigades in line, 44th on the right, 45th on the left. Their objectives will be the BLACK and BLUE lines.
46th Infantry Bde will begin in reserve but will attack the BROWN Line.
12th Div attack on the right of 15th Div. 9th Div on the left.

4. TIMINGS will be approximately:-

Zero plus 40 mins.	arrive BLACK Line.
,, 2 hours	leave ,, ,,
,, 2 h. 40 m.	arrive BLUE Line.
,, 6 h. 40 m.	leave ,, ,,

5. The junction between 44th and 45th Brigades will be between Sapheads 66a and 66b, i.e., about H.24 c.3½.6.
The 70 and 71st Brigades R.F.A. will support the 44th I.B. and will be called the Right sub-group.
The 33rd D.A. supports the 45th I.B. and will be called the left sub-group.

The 45th I.B. will attack with two battalions in line. The 156th Bde R.F.A., supports the right battalion, the 162nd Bde supports the left battalion.

6. Boundaries of 156th Bde.
(a) For bombardment and wire cutting the boundaries of the 156th Brigade will be :-
Right... G.24 d.0.8 - H.19 b.9.1. - H.20 a.3.0, thence along the ARRAS - DOUAI Railway which will be included in 156th Brigade area.
Left.... G.24 a.6½.2 - G.24 a.8½.8½ - G.24 b.3½.8½ - N.W. Corner of FRED'S WOOD - H.19 b.0.7½. - thence along a line running midway between the ARRAS - DOUAI Railway and the River SCARPE. Any points on this line are included in 156th Bde area.

(b) For wire cutting the Right boundary will probably be slightly more to the South.

To sheet 2.

7. Wire Cutting.
   156th Bde has to cut wire at:-

(i) What is known as "F.A" i.e., the wire in front of the support line, and in front of GLOUCESTER TERRACE, about N.24 b.2.1. and N.24 b.3½.1½.
(ii) "F.B" i.e., about N.18 a 3½.4½.
(iii) "E.B" i.e., about N.19 a.6.3½.

B/156 will cut (iii), C/156 will cut (i) and (ii). All gaps as wide as possible and the same batteries will keep the gaps open.
   Ammunition, 200 rounds a day.
   Enough at night to stop repairs by the enemy.

8. Preliminary Bombardment. will continue for 96 hours prior to zero hour on Z day.
   Details will be issued later when the programme is settled, but the programme is a very carefully considered affair, and any battery that skimps its tasks imperils the success of the programme. Reliefs must be arranged as necessary, and atmospheric changes carefully watched for, so that corrections may be made for them.

9. Battery positions.

	FIRST.		SECOND.	
	Number	Approx.Position	Number	Approx.Position.
A	249	N.15 d.9.0.	250	N.23 b.2.0.
B	204	N.21 b.6½.6.	265	N.23 c.3.9½.
C	205	N.21 b.6.2.	262	[illegible]
D	207	N.22 a.5.5.	258	N.23 d.1½.6½.

10. Liason and F.O.O's.
   (a) In principle the following is accepted:-
   Liaison Officers. With H.Q. 48th I.B. Capt.PRIOR and one telephonist with D.III etc.
   with Right Battalion 48th I.B.
   2/Lt. HARVEY and one telephonist with D.III etc.
   They will use communications laid out by 162nd Bde, (156 Bde lends 162 Bde 6 signallers for the purpose).
   (b) Sub-group O.P. at Lydd O.P. No.74.
   2/Lt. BLOOR and two telephonists with instruments.

   All the above are under Sub-group Commander (Capt.STEWART)

11. F.O.O.s. One per battery will go forward with communication staff to Embankment N.15 d. 9. :-
   A 2/Lt. HUGHES.
   B Capt. TAYLOR.
   C 2/Lt
   D 2/Lt GORMAN.
   Detailed orders will be issued later, but in principle A and D form one pair, B and C another.

Lines of Communication.
(a) Each pair will push forward one visual station as quick as possible to the Embankment. One of them signals back to [illegible] SAUVEUR the other to about 23 d.
   French lamps are being asked for to supplement flags etc.
(b) One pair lays a laddered line straight across country from the screened exchange (end of bury) 22 a. 8. to the Embankment.
(c) The other pair lays a laddered line to the R. SCARPE and then a single line along the river to the Embankment.

12. Buffer Springs. Any guns requiring new springs must be sent to I.O.M., 4, RUE DE LILLE near the Brigade's first position.
   Bde.H.Q. will have no spare springs.
   B.C's must make special arrangements to keep on refilling buffers as they leak during the firing; sights, especially range dials, must be tested several times daily during the bombardment and on "Z" day.
   To sheet 3.

S E C R E T.

AMENDMENT No.1 to

Lethal and Lachrymatory Shell Bombardment

by D/156 on "Y" Day.

Time.	Target	Ammunition	Remarks.
Remainder of period Zero -10 hrs to Zero -4 hrs.	(i) & (ii)	725 rds. Lachrymatory	
Remainder of period Zero -3 hrs. to Zero -2 hrs.	(i) & (ii)	125 rds Lachrymatory	
Remainder of period Zero -1 hr. 15 mins. to Zero -15 mins.	(i) & (ii)	300 Lethal.	

April 6th. 1917.

[signature]
Capt. R.F.A.
Adjutant, 156th Brigade R.F.A.

<u>S E C R E T</u>.

<u>Programme of firing "Q" day and "Q/Y" night.</u>

1. "Q" day begins 5 a.m. April 7th.
   "Q/Y" night from 7 p.m. April 7th to 5 a.m. April 8th.

2. By day batteries will

   (a) be tested by Brigade Commander as to firing (programme to follow) B at 9 a.m, C at 11 a.m, D 2 p.m, A 4.p.m. B.C's to meet C.O. at an O.P. to be notified later at these hours. If misty at 9 a.m., B would come at 6 p.m.

   (b) Test their barrages for accuracy.

   (c) Support any raids ordered.

   (d) 18-prs enlarge existing gaps in wire.
       4.5" Hows: bombard as on "V" day.

3. By night.

   18-prs (a) Brigade area in G.24 and whole of H.19
          (b) Prevent repair of wire.

   4.5" Hows: as for W/X night. Firing to be spread over the night as usual.

4. Ammunition for 18-prs, for the 24 hours not to exceed 200 rounds per gun, of which 100 rounds per gund will be fired at night.

   for 4.5" Hows, not to exceed 200 rounds per howitzer.

   Battery Commanders must arrange that at Zero hour on "Z" day they have at least,
   for 18-prs 500 rounds per gun (70% AX, 20% A)
   for 4.5" Hows: 300 rounds BX per gun.

5. No practice barrage.

6. Pauses for photography:-

   12 noon to 12.30 p.m.
   5 p.m. to 5.30 p.m.

April 6th. 1917.

Capt. R.F.A.
Adjutant, 15[illegible]th Brigade R.F.A.

SECRET.

LEFT SUB-GROUP ORDER No. 6.

Reference 15th Divisional Artillery Preliminary Instruction No. 5, Table "A".

1. Batteries will advance by Sections and not as laid down in Table "A".

One Section of each Battery will advance on receipt of an order from this Office.

The second Section of each Battery will not advance until the first Section has registered.

The third Section of each Battery will advance as soon as the second Section opens fire.

Officers Commanding Batteries ~~occupying~~ occupying adjacent forward positions must mutually arrange the moves of their Sections to avoid confusion on the forward positions.

2. Communication will be maintained with the wagon line as follows :-

By telephone to A/156th rear position (via 156th Bde. exchange), thence by flag or cycle orderly to the wagon lines.

Each Brigade will detail an orderly to report to A/156th Brigade rear position at ZERO + 2 hours.

This orderly must know the way to the wagon lines.

3. All N.C.Os. must know the road from the wagon lines to the rear positions, thence to the forward positions and from the latter back to the wagon lines.

4. Teams will be parked in the wagon lines in the order in which they will move off.

5. Acknowledge.

T. E. Durrie

Major, R.A.,
Brigade Major 33rd Divisional Artillery.

7..4.17.

HEADQUARTERS BM 19/49 5 APR 1917 33rd DIV. ARTY.

1 mistake on page 6

BARRAGE SCHEME 18-prs.

LEFT SUB-GROUP.

Time From	Time To	Unit.	Objective	No. of guns	Rate of fire	No. of rounds	Remarks.
ZERO	+4'	156th Bde.	Front line G.24.d.~~00.70~~ 05.65 to G.24.a.87.26.	18	~~2~~ 4 rounds per gun per min.	288 ~~144~~	Shrapnel Long Corrector to give 60% on Graze.
		A/162 Bde.	Trench from G.24.a.87.26 to G.24.a.90.40	6	4 -do-	96 ~~48~~	-ditto-
		B/162nd ,,	G.24.b.05.75 - G.24.b.35.82.	6	4 -do-	96 ~~48~~	-ditto-
		C/162 Bde.	Support line from G.24.d.25.65 to G.24.b.05.65.	6	4 -do-	96 ~~48~~	-ditto-
+4'	+8'	156 Bde.	Support line G.24.d.25.65 to G.24.b.12.35.	18	4 -do-	288 ~~144~~	-ditto-
		A/162 Bde.	G.24.b.12.35 to G.24.b.10.60	6	4 -do-	96 ~~48~~	-ditto-
		B/162 Bde	G.24.b.40.60 to G.24.b.50.90	6	4 -do-	96 ~~48~~	-ditto-
		C/162 Bde.	G.24.d.40.75 to G.24.b.45.60	6	4 -do-	96 ~~48~~	-ditto-
+8'	+16'	156th Bde.	G.24.d.65.75 to G.24.b.55.50	18	3 -do-	432 ~~288~~	-ditto-
		A/162 Bde.	G.24.b.55.50 to G.24.b.60.75	6	3 -do-	144 ~~96~~	-ditto-
+8'	+12'	B/162 Bde.	G.24.b.50.70 to G.24.b.60.90	6	3 -do-	72 ~~48~~	-ditto-
+12' / +16'	~~+20'~~ +16' / +20'	B/162 Bde.	Search forward to line H.13.c.30.15 - H.13.c.25.35.	6	3 -do- / 2 -do-	72 / 48 ~~96~~	-do-
+8'	+12'	C/162 Bde.	G.24.d.65.80 to G.24.b.60.75.	6	3 -do-	72 ~~48~~	-ditto-
+12'	+16'	C/162 Bde	1 Section FRED'S WOOD	2	3 -do-	24 ~~16~~	-ditto-
			2 Sections HUNTINGDON TRENCH from G.24.b.85.80 to H.19.a.35.95.	4	3 -do-	48 ~~32~~	-ditto-

18-prs continued.

Time From	Time To	Unit	Objective	No. of guns	Rate of fire	No. of rounds	Remarks.
+ 16'	+ 20'	156th Bde	G.24.d.95.85 to G.24.b.90.60	18	2 RPGPM.	144	50% shrapnel with long Corrector. 50% H.E. These should be fired by alternate guns.
		A/162 Bde	G.24.b.90.60 to G.24.b.80.85	6	-do-	48	
		B/162 Bde	As above	6	-do-	48	
		C/162 Bde	H.19.a.70.05 to H.19.a.30.90.	6	-do-	48	-do-
+ 20'	+ 24'	156th Bde	H.19.c.20.95 to H.19.a.10.75	18	-do-	144	-do-
		A/162 Bde	H.19.a.10.75 to H.13.c.05.80	6	-do-	48	-do-
		B/162 Bde	As above	6	-do-	48	-do-
		C/162 Bde	1 Section HUNTINGDON TRENCH from H.19.a.37.95 to H.19.b.40.85	2	-do-	16	
			2 Sections RAILWAY from H.19.a.70.00 to H.19.b.40.65.	4	-do-	32.	
						324	
+ 24'	+ 1 hr.	156th Bde	H.19.a.70.00 to H.19.a.40.80	18	½ RPGPM		All H.E.
		A/162 Bde	H.19.a.40.80 to H.13.c.25.10	6	-do-	108	-do-
		B/162 Bde	1 Section H.13.c.25.10 to H.13.c.25.35	2	-do-	36	-do-
			2 Sections enfilade HUNGERFORD ~~TRENCH~~ LANE, OIL TRENCH and HUNTINGDON TRENCH East of H.19.a.37.95.	4	-do-	72	-do-
		C/162 Bde	As above	6	-do-	108	-do-
+ 1 hr.	+ 2 hrs	156th Bde	As ~~above~~ for +24m to +1 hr.	18	1/3 RPGPM	360	-do-
		A/162 Bde	As above	6	-do-	120	-do-
		B/162 Bde	As above	6	-do-	120	-do-
		C/162 Bde	As above	6	-do-	120	-do-
+ 2 hrs	+ 2 hrs 20'	156th Bde	As above	18	½ RPGPM	180	-do-
		A/162 Bde	As above	6	-do-	60	-do-
		B/162 Bde	As above	6	-do-	60	-do-
		C/162 Bde	As above	6	-do-	60	-do-

18-prs continued.

Time From	Time To	Unit	Objective.	No. of guns	Rate of fire	No. of rounds	Remarks.
+2 hrs 20'	+2 hrs 24'	156th Bde	H.19.a.85.10 to H.19.a.65.90	18	2 RPGPM	144	50% Shrapnel with long corrector.
		A/162nd ,,	H.19.a.65.90 to H.13.c.60.20	6	-do-	48	50% H.E.
+2 hrs 20'	+2 hrs 28'	B/162 Bde	Enfilade HUNGERFORD LANE, OIL TRENCH, and HUNTINGDON TRENCH, lifting with the creeping barrage.	6	-do-	96	Alternate guns to fire Shrapnel & H.E -do-
		C/162 Bde.	RAILWAY from H.19.b.50.20 to H.13.d.70.35 and the trenches parallel to it.	6	-do-	96	-do-
+2 hrs 28'	+2 hrs 36'	B/162 Bde.	As above.	6	3 RPGPM	144	-do-
		C/162nd ,,	As above	6	3 R.P.G.P.M.	144	-do-
+2 hrs 24'	+2 hrs 28'	156th Bde	H.19.a.95.10 to H.19.a.90.95	18	2 RPGPM	144	-do-
		?/162 Bde	H.19.a.90.95 to H.13.c.90.20	6	-do-	48	-do-
+2 hrs 28'	+2 hrs 32'	156th Bde.	H.19.b.20.15 to H.19.b.20.95. A B/C	18	3 RPGPM A & B/156 2 RPGPM C/156	216	-do-
		A/162 Bde	H.19.b.20.95 to H.13.d.15.25	6	-do-	72	-do-
+2 hrs 32'	+2 hrs 36'	156th Bde.	H.19.b.37.17 to H.19.b.40.97 A+B 3 RPGPM	18	~~-do-~~	216	-do-
		A/162 Bde	H.19.b.40.97 to H.13.d.40.20 C 2 RPGPM	6	-do-	72	-do-
+2 hrs 36'	+2 hrs 40'	156th Bde.	H.19.b.60.20 to H.13.d.70.05	18	~~-do-~~ 2 R.P.G.P.M.	216	-do-
		A/162 Bde	H.13.d.70.05 to H.13.d.70.35	6	-do-	72	-do-
+2 hrs 36'	+2 hrs 40'	B/162 Bde.	Thoroughly search WATERY WOOD and ground between it and the River.	6	3 RPGPM	72	-do-
		C/162 Bde.	Trench H.20.a.25.00 - H.20.a.90.10 - H.20.a.30.30 Trench H 20 A 60.20 to H 20 C 55-95	6	-do-	72	-do-
+2 hrs 40'	+2 hrs 56'	B/162 Bde	As above	6	2 RPGPM	192	-do-
		C/162 Bde	As above	6	-do-	192	-do-

18pr's continued.

Time From		Unit	Objective.	No. of guns	Rate of fire	No. of rounds	Remarks.
+2 hrs 40'	+2 hrs 44'	156th Bde.	H.19.d.85.95 to H.19.b.95.95	18	2 RPGPM	144	50% shrapnel with long corrector.
		A/162 Bde	H.19.b.95.95 to H.14.c.00.30	6	-do-	48	50% H.E. Alternate guns to fire shrapnel & H.E
+2 hrs 44'	+2 hrs 56'	156th Bde.	H.20.c.05.95 to H.20.a.15.95	18	-do-	432	~~All H.E.~~ Ditto
		A/162 Bde.	H.20.a.15.95 to H.14.c.25.30	6	-do-	144	,,
+2 hrs 56'	+2 hrs 58'	156th Bde.	H.20.c.25.95 to H.20.a.35.70	13	-do-	72	50% Shrapnel 50% HE etc.
		A/162 Bde.	H.20.a.35.70 to H.20.a.35.95	6	-do-	24	
+2 hrs 56'	+3 hrs 2'	B/162 Bde.	Search forward to and remain on the area H.21.a.2.5. - H.21.a.2.8. H.20.b.8.5. - H.20.b.8.9.	6	2 RPGPM	72	All H.E.
		C/162 Bde.	FEUCHY LANE from H.20.b.20.05. to H.20.d.80.75.	6	-do-	72	-do-
+3 hrs 2'	+ 4 hrs 30'	B/162 Bde	As above	6	½ RPGPM	264	-do-
		C/162 Bde	As above	6	-do-	264	-do-
+4 hrs 30'	+ 5 hrs 45'	B/162 Bde	As above	6	1/3 RPGPM	150	-do-
		C/162 Bde.	As above	6	-do-	150	-do-
+5 hrs 45'	+ 6 hrs 40'	B/~~156~~ 162 Bde.	As above	6	½ RPGPM	165	-do-
		C/162 Bde.	As above	6	-do-	165	-do-
+2 hrs 58'	+ 3 hrs	156th Bde.	H.20.c.45.95 to H.20.a.50.40.	18	2 RPGPM	72	50% Shrapnel 50% H.E
		A/162 Bde.	H.20.a.50.40 to H.20.a.55.60	6	-do-	24	-do-
+3 hrs	+3 hrs 2'	156th Bde.	H.20.c.70.95 to H.20.a.75.30.	18	-do-	72	-do-
		A/162 Bde.	H.20.a.75.30 to H.20.a.75.40.	6	-do-	24	-do-
+3 hrs 2'	+4 hrs 30'	156th Bde.	H.20.d.00.90 to H.20.b.00.25	18	½ RPGPM	792	All H.E.
		A/162 Bde.	H.20.b.00.25 to H.20.b.10.40	6	-do-	264	-do-

Time From	Time to	Unit	Objective.	No. of guns	Rate of fire	No. of rounds	Remarks.
+ 4 hrs 30'	+ 5 hrs 45'	156th Bde.	H.20.d.00.90 to H.20.b.00.25 c.35.60	18	1/3 RPGPM	450	All H.E.
		A/162 Bde.	H.20.b.00.25 to H.20.b.10.40	6	-do-	150	-do-
							3/4 hr. Pause.
+ 5 hrs 45'	+ 6 hrs 40'	156th Bde.	As above for + 4h 30m to + 5h 45'	18	½ RPGPM	495	-do-
		A/162 Bde.	As above	6	-do-	165	-do-
+ 6 hrs 40'	+ 6 hrs 42'	156th Bde.	H.20.d.25.60 to H.20.b.25.20.	18	2 RPGPM	72	50% Shrapnel 50% H.E
		A/162 Bde.	H.20.b.25.20 to H.20.b.25.40	6	-do-	24	-do-
+ 6 hrs 40'	+ 6 hrs 48'	B/162 Bde.	As before	6	-do-	96	-do-
		C/162 Bde	FEUCHY WORK.	6	-do-	96	-do-
+ 6 hrs 42'	+ 6 hrs 44'	156th Bde.	H.20.d.45.65 to H.20.b.45.20	18	-do-	72	-do-
		A/162 Bde.	H.20.b.45.20 to H.20.b.45.35	6	-do-	24	-do-
+ 6 hrs 44'	+ 6 hrs 46'	156th Bde.	H.20.d.65.65 to H.20.b.65.15	18	-do-	72	-do-
		A/162 Bde.	H.20.b.65.15 to H.20.b.65.35	6	-do-	24	-do-
+ 6 hrs 46'	+ 6 hrs 48'	156th Bde.	H.20.d.87.63 to H.20.b.85.05.	18	-do-	72	-do-
		A/162 Bde.	H.20.b.85.05 to H.20.b.85.20	6	-do-	24	-do-
+ 6 hrs 48'	+ 6 hrs 51	156th Bde.	H.21.c.10.60 to H.21.a.10.30.	18	-do-	108	-do-
		A/162 Bde.	H.21.b.10.30 to H.21.b.10.50	6	-do-	36	-do-
		B/162 Bde.	H.21.b.10.50 to H.21.b.10.70	6	-do-	36	-do-
+ 6 hrs 48'	+ 7 hrs	C/162 Bde.	Area H.21.c.60.80, H.21.a.90.30, H.21.d.50.95, H.21.d.30.55.	6	-do-	144	-do-
+ 6 hrs 51'	+ 6 hrs 54'	156th Bde.	H.21.c.33.55 to H.21.a.27.25	18	-do-	108	-do-
		A/162 Bde.	H.21.a.27.25 to H.21.a.27.50	6	-do-	36	-do-
		B/162 Bde.	H.21.a.27.50 to H.21.a.27.75	6	-do-	36	-do-

18-prs continued.

Time From	Time To	Unit	Objective	No. of guns	Rate of fire	No. of rounds	Remarks
+ 6 hrs 54'	+ 6 hrs 57'	156th Bde	H.21.c.55.45 to H.21.a.50.10.	18	2 RPGPM	108	50% Shrapnel 50% H.E
		A/162 Bde	H.21.a.50.10 to H.21.a.50.30.	6	-do-	36	-do-
		B/162 Bde	H.21.a.50.30 to H.21.a.50.60.	6	-do-	36	-do-
+ 6 hrs 57'	+ 7 hrs	156th Bde	H.21.c.70.35 to H.21.c.70.95.	18	-do-	108	-do-
		A/162 Bde	H.21.c.70.95 to H.21.a.70.20.	6	-do-	36	-do-
		B/162 Bde	Will search the ground between a line H.~~20~~ 21.a.70.35 - H.21.d.50.95 and the river.	6	-do-	36	-do-
+ 7 hrs	+ 7 hrs 55'	156th Bde 162nd Bde	As ~~above~~ fm + 6h 57' to + 7h	36	1 RPGPM	1980	All H.E.

Checked -

18-prs continued.

Time From	Time To	Unit	Objective	No. of guns	Rate of fire	No. of rounds	Remarks.
+ 7 hrs 55'	+ 7 hrs 59'	156th Bde.	H.21.c.95.35 to H.21.c.95.95.	18	2 RPGPM	144	50% A 50% AX
		A/162 Bde	H.21.c.95.95 to H.21.a.95.15.	6	-do-	48	-do-
		C/162 Bde	H.21.a.95.15 to H.21.a.95.35	6	-do-	48	-do-
		B/158 Bde.	H.21.a.95.35 to River SCARPE.	6	-do-	48	-do-
+ 7 hrs 59'	+ 8 hrs 3'	156th Bde.	H.21.d.15.20 to H.21.d.15.80	18	-do-	144	-do-
		A/162 Bde.	H.21.d.15.80 to H.21.b.15.00.	6	-do-	48	-do-
		C/162 Bde.	H.21.b.15.00 to H.21.b.15.20.	6	-do-	48	-do-
		B/162 Bde.	H.21.b.15.20 to River SCARPE.	6	-do-	48	-do-
+ 8 hrs 3'	+ 8 hrs 7'	156th Bde.	H.21.d.33.10 to H.21.d.35.70.	18	-do-	144	-do-
		A/162 Bde.	H.21.d.35.70 to H.21.d.35.90	6	-do-	48	-do-
		C/162 Bde.	H.21.d.35.90 to H.21.b.35.10.	6	-do-	48	-do-
		B/162 Bde.	H.21.b.35.10 to River SCARPE.	6	-do-	48	-do-
+ 8 hrs 7'	+ 8 hrs 11'	156th Bde.	H.27.b.60.95 to H.21.d.55.55.	18	-do-	144	-do-
		A/162 Bde.	H.21.d.55.55 to H.21.d.55.75.	6	-do-	48	-do-
		C/162 Bde.	H.21.d.55.75 to H.21.d.55.95.	6	-do-	48	-do-
		B/162 Bde.	H.21.d.55.95 to River SCARPE.	6	-do-	48	-do-
+ 8 hrs 11'	+ 8 hrs 15'	156th Bde.	H.27.b.80.95 to H.21.d.80.55.	18	-do-	144	-do-
		A/162 Bde.	H.21.d.80.55 to H.21.d.80.75	6	-do-	48	-do-
		C/162 Bde.	H.21.d.80.75 to H.21.d.80.95	6	-do-	48	-do-
		B/162 Bde.	H.21.d.80.95 to River SCARPE.	6	-do-	48	-do-
+ 8 hrs 15'	+ 8 hrs 19'	156th Bde.	H.28.a.00.90 to H.22.c.00.50	18	-do-	144	-do-
		A/162 Bde.	H.22.c.00.50 to H.22.c.00.70.	6	-do-	48	-do-
		C/162 Bde.	H.22.c.00.70 to H.22.c.00.90.	6	-do-	48	-do-
		B/162 Bde.	H.22.c.00.90 to River SCARPE.	6	-do-	48	-do-
+ 8 hrs 19'	+ 8 hrs 23'	156th Bde.	H.28.a.20.85 to H.22.c.20.35.	18	-do-	144	-do-
		A/162 Bde.	H.22.c.20.35 to H.22.c.20.55	6	-do-	48	-do-
		C/162 Bde.	H.22.c.20.55 to H.22.c.20.75	6	-do-	48	-do-
		B/162 Bde.	H.22.c.20.75 to River SCARPE.	6	-do-	48	-do-

"A" Form.

MESSAGES AND SIGNALS.

Army Form C.2121 (in pads of 100).

No. of Message

Prefix ... Code ... m. | Words | Charge | This message is on a/c of: ... Service. | Recd. at ... m.

Office of Origin and Service Instructions. Secret

Sent At ... m. To ... By ...

(Signature of "Franking Officer.")

Date ... From ... By ...

TO ~~PULPIT~~ PAINT

Sender's Number.	Day of Month.	In reply to Number.	AAA
*BM 19/49			

Correction to Barrage Scheme 18 prs.

Page 7 7 hrs 55 to 7 hrs 59 read
H 21 c 95 35 to H 21 c 95 95
H 21 c 95 95 to H 21 a 95 15
H 21 a 95 15 to H 21 a 95 35
H 21 a 95 35 to River

T E Durie
Major
R.F.A

From

Place

Time

The above may be forwarded as now corrected. (Z)

Censor. Signature of Addressor or person authorised to telegraph in his name.

* This line should be erased if not required.

K0.306. W 3186—M509. H. W. & V., Ld. 6/16.

18prs continued.

Time From	Time To	Unit	Objectivo	No. of guns	Rate of fire	No. of rounds	Remarks.
+8 hrs 23'	+9 hrs	A/156 Bde	H 28.a.40.80 to H.28.a.55.80 to H 28.a 55 90	6	3 RPGPM	666	50% A 50% AX
		B/156 Bde	H 28.a 40 90 to H.28.a.55.90 to H 22.c.55.00	6	-do-	666	-do-
		C/156 Bde	H.22 c 55.00 to H.22 c 55.25	6	-do-	666	-do-
		A/162 Bde	H.22.c.55 25 to H.22.c.55.50	6	-do-	666	-do-
		C/162 Bde	H.22.c.55 50 to H.22 c.60 75	6	-do-	666	-do-
		B/162 Bde	H.22.c 60 75 to River	6	-do-	666	-do-
+9 hrs	+9 hrs 2'	A/156 Bde.	H.28.a.70.75 to H.28 A 70.90	6	-do-	36	-do-
		B/156 Bde.	H.28.a.70.90 to H 22.c 70.05	6	-do-	36	-do-
		C/156 Bde.	H.22 c 70.05 to H.22 c.70.20.	6	-do-	36	-do-
		A/162 Bde.	H.22.c 70 18 to H 22 c 75 40	6	-do-	36	-do-
		C/162 Bde.	H 22.c 75 40 to H 22.c 75.75	6	-do-	36	-do-
		B/162 Bde	H 22.c.75.75 to River.	6	-do-	36	-do-
+9 hrs 2'	+9 hrs 4'	156th Bde	H.28 a 95 80 to H 22 c 95.25	18	½ RPGPM	18	All H.E.
		A/162 Bde	H.22 c 95 25 to H.22.c.95.40	6	-do-	6	-do-
		C/162 Bde	H.22.c 95 40 to H 22 c.95.75	6	-do-	6	-do-
		B/162 Bde.	H 22 c.95.75 to River.	6	-do-	6	-do-
+9 hrs 4'	+9 hrs 6'	156th Bde.	H.28.b.40.85 to H 22.d 40.15.	18	-do-	18	-do-
		A/162 Bde.	H.22 d 40 15 to H 22 d 40.25	6	-do-	6	-do-
		C/162 Bde.	H.22.d 40 25 to H.22.d 40.35	6	-do-	6	-do-
		B/162 Bde.	H.22.d.40.35 to River.	6	-do-	6	-do-
+9 hrs 6'	+9 hrs 8'	156th Bde.	H.28.b.75.95 to H.22.d.75.30.	18	-do-	16	-do-
		A/162 Bde.	H.22.d.75.30 to H.22.d.75.40	6	-do-	6	-do-
		C/162 Bde.	H.22.d.75.40 to H.22.d.75.50	6	-do-	6	-do-
		B/162 Bde.	H.22.b.75.00 to River.	6	-do-	6	-do-

18prs continued.

Time From	Time To	Unit	Objective	No. of guns	Rate of fire	No. of rounds	Remarks.
+9 hrs 8'	+9 hrs 10'	156th Bde.	H.23.c.00.00 to H.23.c.00.45	18	½ RPGPM	18	All H.E.
		A/162 Bde.	H.23.c.00.45 to H.23.c.00.55	6	-do-	6	-do-
		C/162 Bde.	H.23.c.00.55 to H.23.c.00.65	6	-do-	6	-do-
		B/162 Bde.	H.23.a.00.10 to River	6	-do-	6	-do-
+9 hrs 10'	+9 hrs 12'	156th Bde.	H.23.c.55.10 to H.23.c.45.65	18	1/3 RPGPM	12	-do-
		A/162 Bde.	H.23.c.45.65 to H.23.c.45.80	6	-do-	4	-do-
		C/162 Bde.	H.23.c.45.80 to H.23.c.40.95	6	-do-	4	-do-
		B/162 Bde.	H.23.c.40.95 to River.	6	-do-	4	-do-
+9 hrs 12'	+9 hrs 14'	156th Bde.	H.23.c.90.10 to H.23.c.80.80.	18	-do-	12	-do-
		A/162 Bde.	H.23.c.80.80 to H.23.a.75.00	6	-do-	4	-do-
		C/162 Bde.	H.23.a.75.00 to H.23.a.75.20	6	-do-	4	-do-
		B/162 Bde.	H.23.a.75.20 to River.	6	-do-	4	-do-
+9 hrs 14'	Onwards	156th Bde.	H.23.d.70.45 to H.23.b.35.10.	18	-		-do-
		A/162 Bde.	H.23.b.35.10 to H.23.b.27.20	6			-do-
		C/162 Bde.	H.23.b.27.20 to H.23.b.15.43	6			-do-
		B/162 Bde.	H.23.b.15.43 to H.23.a.95.70	6			-do-

In this programme "As above" refers to the last order of the same Battery and not to the last co-ordinates mentioned.

Batteries barraging through Railway Triangle will fire 3 R.P.G.P.M. while passing through the Triangle.

When the ammunition allotted is 50% A 50% AX, alternate guns will fire A or AX to avoid confusion.

156

33rd D.A.
B.M. 19/49.

CORRECTIONS TO LEFT SUB-GROUP BARRAGE SCHEME.

18prs.

Page 4.	2 hrs 44' to 2 hrs 56'	Delete "All H.E." and substitute " "-ditto-"
Page 4	5 hrs 45' to 6 hrs 40'	For "B/156" read "B/162".
Page 5	4 hrs 30' to 5 hrs 45'	156th Bde. for "H.20.d.00.90" read "H.20.c.95.60".
Page 5	6 hrs 48' to 6 hrs 51'	For "H.21.b." read "H.21.a."
Page 6	6 hrs 57 to 7 hrs	B/162 Bde. for "H.20.a." read "H.21.a"

4.5" Howitzers.

Page 1	4' to 8'	For "G.24.b.55.20" read "G.24.b.40.20
Page 1	8' to 12'	For "G.24.b.70.25" read "G.24.b.60.25

Herewith 5 copies of pages 7, 8 and 9 for 18prs and page 4 for 4.5" howitzers.

Please acknowledge.

T E Durie
Major, R.A.,
Brigade Major 33rd Divisional Artillery.

6.4.17.

BARRAGE SCHEME.

4.5" Howitzers

Time From	Time To	Unit.	Objective.	No. of Hows	Rate of fire	No. of rounds	Remarks.
ZERO	+4'	D/156 Bde.	Support line from G.24.d.25.65 to G.24.b.20.15.	6	2 rounds per How. per min.	48	Special attention to be paid to trench junctions and any known M.G. or T.M. emplacem
		D/162 Bde.	Support line from G.24.b.20.15 to G.24.b.05.60.	6	-do-	48	-ditto-
+4'	+8'	D/156 Bde.	GLOUCESTER TERRACE from G.24.d.40.75 to G.24.b.~~55.20~~ 40.20	6	-do-	48	-ditto-
		D/162 Bde.	GLOUCESTER TERRACE from G.24.b.55.20 to G.24.b.40.60.	6	-do-	48	-ditto-
+8'	+12'	D/156 Bde	GOSFORD TERRACE from G.24.d.65.80 to G.24.b.~~80~~ 60.25.	6	-do-	48	-ditto-
		D/162 Bde.	GOSFORD TERRACE from G.24.b.~~45~~ 60.25 to G.24.b.60.75.	6	-do-	48	-ditto-
+12'	+16'	D/156 Bde.	FRED'S WOOD	6	-do-	48	-do-
		D/162 Bde.	HUNTINGDON TRENCH from G.24.b.85.80 to H.19.a.35.95.	6	-do-	48	-do-
+16'	+20'	D/156 Bde.	HALF TRENCH from H.19.a.70.00 to H.19.a.55.45.	6	-do-	48	-do-
		D/162 Bde.	HALF TRENCH from H.19.a.55.45 to H.19.a.35.95.	6	-do-	48	-do-

4.5" Howitzers continued.

Time From	Time To	Unit	Objective	No. of guns	Rate of fire	No. of rounds	Remarks.
+ 20'	+ 24'	D/156 Bde.	RAILWAY from H.19.a.70.00 to H.19.b.40.65	6	1 RPGPM	24	Special attention to be paid to trench junctions and any known M.G or T.M. emplacements.
		D/162 Bde.	HUNTINGDON TRENCH from H.19.a.35.95 to H.19.b.40.85.	6	-do-	24	
+ 24'	+ 1 hr.	D/156 Bde.	As ~~above~~ for + 20" to + 24"	6	½ RPGPM	108	
		D/162 Bde.	As above	6	-do-	108	
+ 1 hr.	+ 2 hrs	D/156 Bde.	As ~~above~~ for + 20" to + 24"	6	1/3 RPGPM	120	-do-
		D/162 Bde	As above	6	-do-	120	-do-
+ 2 hrs	+ 2 hrs 20'	D/156 Bde.	As ~~above~~ for + 20" to + 24"	6	½ RPGPM	60	-do-
		D/162 Bde.	As above	6	-do-	60	-do-
+ 2 hrs 20'	+ 2 hrs 36'	D/156 Bde.	RAILWAY and Trenches along it from H.19.b.50.20 to H.19.b.50.85	6	2 RPGPM	192	Paying particular attention to trench junctions & strong points.
		D/162 Bde.	RAILWAY and trenches along it from H.19.b.50.85 to H.13.d.70.35.	6	-do-	192	
+ 2 hrs 36'	+ 2 hrs 56'	D/156 Bde.	Trench H.20.a.25.00 to H.20.a.90.10	6	-do-	240	Particular attention to H.20.a.30.10
		D/162 Bde.	FEUCHY LANE from H.20.a.90.10 to H.20.a.30.30.	4	-do-	160	Particular attention to trench junct.
			Trench from H.20.a.60.20 to H.20.c.55.95	2	-do-	80	-do-
+ 2 hrs 56'	+ 3 hrs 2'	D/156 Bde.	FEUCHY LANE from H.20.d.80.75 to H.20.b.55.00.	6	-do-	72	
		D/162 Bde.	FEUCHY LANE from H.20.b.55.00 to H.20.b.20.05.	6	-do-	72	
+ 3 hrs 2'	+ 4 hrs 30'	D/156 Bde.	As above	6	½ RPGPM	264	
		D/162 Bde.	As above	6	-do-	264	
+ 4 hrs 30'	+ 5 hrs 45'	D/156 Bde.	As above	6	1/3 RPGPM	210	
		D/162 Bde.	As above	6	-do-	210	

4.5" howitzers continued.

Time From	Time To	Unit	Objective	No. of guns	Rate of fire	No. of rounds	Remarks.
+ 5 hrs 45'	+ 6 hrs 40'	D/156 Bde.	FEUCHY LANE from H.20.d.80.75 to H.20.b.55.00	6	½ RPGPM	165	
		D/162 Bde.	FEUCHY LANE from H.20.b.55.00 to H.20.b.20.05.	6	-do-	165	
+ 6 hrs 40'	+ 6 hrs 48'	D/156 Bde.	Area H.20.d.85.75, H.20.b.95.00, H.21.a.23.07, H.21.c.25.55	6	2 RBGPM	96	Particular attention to trench junctions.
		D/162 Bde.	Area H.20.b.95.00, H.21.a.05.85 H.21.a.30.75, H.21.a.50.25.	6	-do-	96	Particular attention to houses.
+ 6 hrs 48'	+ 7 hrs.	D/156 Bde.	Area H.21.c.60.80, H.21.a.75.05. H.21.d.30.55.	6	-do-	124	-do-
		D/162 Bde.	Area H.21.a.75.05, H.21.a.90.30. H.21.d.50.95, H.21.d.30.55.	6	-do-	144	-do-
+ 7 hrs	+ 7 hrs 55'	D/156 Bde	As ~~above~~ for + 6h 48m to + 7h	6	1 RPGPM	330	-do-
		D/162 Bde.	As above	6	-do-	330	-do-

Checked RB

4.5" Howitzers continued.

Time From	Time To	Unit	Objective	No of guns	Rate of fire	No. of rounds	Remarks.
+7 hrs 55'	+7 hrs 59'	D/156 Bde.	H.21 d.15.15 to H.21.d.15.70.	6	2 RPGPM	48	
		D/162 Bde.	H.21.d.15.70 to H.21.b.15.20.	6	-do-	48	
+7 hrs 59'	+8 hrs 3'	D/156 Bde.	H.21.d 35 10 to H 21.d.35.50.	6	-do-	48	
		D/162 Bde.	H.21.d.35 50 to H 21.d.35.90	6	-do-	48	
+8 hrs 3'	+8 hrs 7'	D/156 Bde	H.21.d 55.00 to H.21 d 55.35.	6	-do-	48	
		D/162 Bde.	H.21.d 55 35 to H 21 d 55.70	6	-do-	48	
+8 hrs 7'	+8 hrs 11'	D/156 Bde.	H 27 b.80 90 to H 21 d 80 20	6	-do-	48	
		D/162 Bde.	H.21.d.80.20 to H 21 d 80.50	6	-do-	48	
+8 hrs 11'	+8 hrs 50'	D/156 Bde.	HIMALAYA TRENCH front line from H.28.a.40.50 to H 28 a 40.95. Trench from H 28 a 20.95 to H.28.a.55.90.	6	-do-	468	
		D/162 Bde.	Trench H.28.a.55 90 H.22.c.55.17. H.22.c 75 18, H 28.a.70.80.	6	-do-	468	
+8 hrs 50'	+8 hrs 55'	D/156 Bde.	Trench H.28.a 55 40 to H.28.a.55.90	6	½ RPGPM	15	
		D/162 Bde.	Trench H.28.a 70 80 to H.28.a.70.90	6	-do-	15	
+8 hrs 55'	+9 hrs 30'	D/156 Bde.	Barrage the Southern bank of the SCARPE H.23.a.00.30 to H 23.b 20.70	6	-do-	105	
		D/162 Bde.	H.23 b 20.75 to H.24.a.20.95.	6	-do-	105	
+9 hrs 30'	Onwards	D/156 Bde.	As ~~above~~ for +8h 55m to +9h 30m	6	1/3 RPGPM		
		D/162 Bde.	As above	6	-do-		

Instructions regarding War Diaries and Intelligence Summaries are contained in F. S. Regs., Part II. and the Staff Manual respectively. Title pages will be prepared in manuscript.

MAY 1917.

WAR DIARY
or
~~INTELLIGENCE SUMMARY.~~
(Erase heading not required.)

136th Brigade RFA

Army Form C. 2118.

33rd

Vol 16

Place	Date	Hour	Summary of Events and Information	Remarks and references to Appendices
(ARRAS) N. of Feuchy	1st		The Brigade took part in an operation to gain the whole of RIFLE TRENCH. The operation was to all intents and purposes a failure. We managed to hold 65 yards of the trench & to establish a block.	Ref. Map FAMPOUX 1:20,000.
	3rd	3.45a	The 1st, 3rd & 5th Armies all attacked simultaneously on this day and at this time, on a front extending from [illegible] down to BULLECOURT. The attacks were successful on many parts of the front. On our immediate front, the Brigade put down a standing barrage on the enemy's front line for three minutes & then began to creep back at the rate of 100 yards per 3 minutes. The first assaulting wave of Infantry followed up the barrage to a line I.25.D.7.7. to GUN TRENCH. Owing to the zero hour being fixed for an hour of darkness all communication between this and the succeeding waves was lost. The second wave managed to reach SCABBARD TRENCH, but were unable to proceed owing to hostile machine gun fire. They finally all retired to the ~~the~~ original front line & the first wave were entirely cut off.	
		12.15p	It was decided to organise a new attack.	
		2.15p	The enemy left SCABBARD TRENCH owing to a very severe barrage of four batteries of 4.5" Howitzer alone. The infantry crept up close under this barrage.	

MAY 1917 (contd. 2) **WAR DIARY** ~~or~~ ~~INTELLIGENCE SUMMARY.~~ 156th Brigade RFA

Army Form C. 2118.

Instructions regarding War Diaries and Intelligence Summaries are contained in F. S. Regs., Part II. and the Staff Manual respectively. Title pages will be prepared in manuscript.

(*Erase heading not required.*)

Place	Date	Hour	Summary of Events and Information	Remarks and references to Appendices
FEUCHY (nr ARRAS)	3rd	2.14	The enemy fled down the bank running eastwards from H.25.c.6.9. were sniped at from the Brigade forward guns in H.23.d.95.70 We then occupied SCABBARD TRENCH on our immediate front	Ref. Map FEUCHY 1:20,000.
		2.15	The enemy made a counter attack on the portion of SCABBARD TRENCH held by us. He failed in this & left several prisoners in our hands. While the fight lasted, the batteries were engaged in firing on the enemy, who were attempting to mass for further counter-attacks, in the dip in the ground behind KEELING COPSE.	
	4th	–	2/Lieut. (A/Captain) C.E. BURRIDGE, 13th Reserve Regiment of Cavalry, was posted to the Brigade. On his arrival he assumed the duties of Staff Officer in charge of Brigade Wagon Lines.	
	5th	–	2/Lieut. T. McC. HANNA was posted to the Brigade from the 3rd Army School of Instruction. He was posted to C.136.	
	11th/12th		An attack was made by the 4th Division, immediately North of the RIVER SCARPE, on the CHEMICAL WORKS and ROEUX CEMETERY. The Brigade stood by, watching for fleeting opportunity targets on our own front. The attack proved to be a success. Over 300 prisoners were taken.	

May 1917 (contd. 3)

Instructions regarding War Diaries and Intelligence Summaries are contained in F. S. Regs., Part II. and the Staff Manual respectively. Title pages will be prepared in manuscript.

WAR DIARY
or
INTELLIGENCE SUMMARY.
(Erase heading not required.)

Army Form C. 2118.

156th Brigade RFA

Place	Date	Hour	Summary of Events and Information	Remarks and references to Appendices
FEUCHY Nr ARRAS.	12/13th	6.45p	An attack was organised to capture DEVILS TRENCH. At Zero Hour the Brigade assisted in putting down a barrage on the enemy's front line for three minutes & then lifted backwards until it rested on the enemy's support line. The infantry followed up the barrage, but were held up 50 yards from DEVILS TRENCH.	Ref. Map FEUCHY 1:20,000.
		10.45p	The Brigade F.O.O. (2/Lieut. R.M. WINGFIELD) who was with the Infantry Company Commander at RIFLE FARM, informed the Brigade H.Q. that the Infantry wanted to rush the trench then. Accordingly at 10.45p the Artillery covering the front put down a barrage on DEVILS TRENCH for 15 minutes & then lifted, & the Infantry assaulted. However, owing to darkness & the exhausted condition of the Infantry, the trench was only assaulted here & there & the situation became quite obscure. By midnight it was reported that our Infantry were all back in our original front line.	
	14th	6p	A Chinese Bombardment was carried out on DEVILS TRENCH. The barrage started on the trench; then crept back, by lifts of 100 yards per three minutes, for 300 yards. It was then brought back on to the trench again for 6 minutes. The barrage was reported to have been a good one.	

2353 Wt. W2544/1454 700,000 5/15 D. D. & L. A.D.S.S./Forms/C. 2118.

May 1917 (contd. 4)

155th Brigade R.F.A.

Army Form C. 2118.

Instructions regarding War Diaries and Intelligence Summaries are contained in F. S. Regs., Part II. and the Staff Manual respectively. Title pages will be prepared in manuscript.

WAR DIARY
or
~~INTELLIGENCE~~ SUMMARY.

(Erase heading not required.)

Place	Date	Hour	Summary of Events and Information	Remarks and references to Appendices
FEUCHY (ARRAS)	15th	1am	During the previous few nights, the batteries had kept up a desultory fire on the road running due East from PELVES towards HAMBLAIN. Accordingly, the aeroplane photos showed tracks running parallel to & 150 yards south of this road, & the tracks became plainer every day. At 10pm on the 15th inst. the road was shelled until 1am when a barrage was put up & down the tracks running parallel to it, in order to catch the traffic. The enemy shelled our lines of communication heavily the next day & night which would point to the above barrage causing them much annoyance.	Ref. Map [illegible] 1/20,000
	16th	3am	The enemy bombarded the front immediately North of the Scarpe all day on the 15th inst., & the valleys of FEUCHY, and back areas in general received attention. At 3.am 16th the enemy attacked our positions East of the CHEMICAL WORKS and ROEUX CEMETERY which we gained on the 12th May 17. Our infantry were driven out.	
		8.30am	It was reported that we had counter attacked & retaken our positions.	
		9.30am	The enemy counter attacked but was driven off & after fighting all day, we were still in the positions we had gained on the 12th inst. by night fall.	
	16th		Captain J.K. SMALL RAMC assumed duties of M.O. i/c Brigade vice Captain W.L. [illegible] RAMC who proceeded to the Base	

#353 Wt. W2544/1454 700,000 5/15 D. D. & L. A.D.S.S./Forms/C. 2118.

May 1917 (contd. 5) **WAR DIARY** 156th Brigade R.F.A. Army Form C. 2118.

or

~~INTELLIGENCE SUMMARY.~~

(Erase heading not required.)

Instructions regarding War Diaries and Intelligence Summaries are contained in F. S. Regs., Part II. and the Staff Manual respectively. Title pages will be prepared in manuscript.

Place	Date	Hour	Summary of Events and Information	Remarks and references to Appendices
FEUCHY (nr ARRAS)	17th	-	Captain C.E. BEERBOHM was posted to the Brigade.	Ref MAP FAMPOUX. 1:20,000.
	18th	-	Captain (A/Major) G. LOMER was struck off the strength, being retained at home owing to illness. C.156.	
			2/Lieut. C.G. BARLOW. B.156. died of wounds.	
	19th	-	An attack was organised on the Southern Portion of DEVIL'S TRENCH and on TOOL TRENCH. The Brigade assisted in the flank barrage for 60 minutes & then stood by. Our infantry succeeded in gaining a footing in TOOL TRENCH but were bombed out & had to retire to their original front line.	
	23rd	-	Captain (A/Major) A. BARKER was posted to the Brigade and was posted to command C/156.	
	25th	-	2/Lieut. N. GRANT B.156 was killed in action.	
	30th/31st	11.30p	An attack was organised on the portion of HOOK TRENCH still held by the enemy. The Brigade switched southwards to assist in the barrage, the 34th Division, north of the River, switching southwards also to cover the former Brigade zone. The enemy saw our Infantry leave the trenches, immediately opened up a heavy barrage of Machine Gun & Artillery fire. Two officers & 40 men succeeded in getting in to the trench, but were overcome later by superior forces of the enemy.	

2353 Wt. W2544/1454 700,000 5/15 D. D. & L. A.D.S.S./Forms/C. 2118.

Army Form C. 2118.

May 1917 (contd. 6) **WAR DIARY** 156th Brigade RFA

or

INTELLIGENCE SUMMARY.

(Erase heading not required.)

Instructions regarding War Diaries and Intelligence Summaries are contained in F. S. Regs., Part II. and the Staff Manual respectively. Title pages will be prepared in manuscript.

Place	Date	Hour	Summary of Events and Information	Remarks and references to Appendices
FEUCHY (Nr. ARRAS)	30th/31st	-	Our infantry were forced to retire and to re-occupy their original front line. At 11.30 p while this attack was in progress, the left Battalion of the 88th Infantry Brigade made an attempt to rush & capture a German trench running from I.25.c.3.2. to I.25.D.4.9. to I.25.D.50.70 This attack failed, but they succeeded in establishing a post at I.25.D.55.60.	Ref. Map FEUCHY 1:20,000.
			CASUALTIES. During the month of May 1917. Killed Wounded Officers. 2. - Other Ranks. 8. 22	
			B. Butler Lieut. Col. Commanding 156th Brigade RFA	

2353 Wt. W2544/1454 700,000 5/15 D. D. & L. A.D.S.S./Forms/C. 2118.

(3)

156th Brigade R.F.A.

WAR DIARY
or
INTELLIGENCE SUMMARY.
(Erase heading not required.)

June 1917 (contd) — Army Form C. 2118.

Instructions regarding War Diaries and Intelligence Summaries are contained in F. S. Regs., Part II. and the Staff Manual respectively. Title pages will be prepared in manuscript.

Place	Date	Hour	Summary of Events and Information	Remarks and references to Appendices
IN THE FIELD HENIN.	30/5/17		Captain H. Tayler, B/156, was evacuated sick to England.	
	3/6/17		2/Lieut. A. D. McEwan rejoined the Brigade, and was posted to C/156.	
	4/6/17		2/Lieut. G. W. Williamson, C/156, was evacuated sick to England.	
	13/6/17		2/Lieut. V. A. Barsham joined the Brigade and was posted to B/156	
	14/6/17		2/Lieut. H. B. Molyneux joined the Brigade and was posted to B/156	
	15/6/17		2/Lieut. F. W. Beadle joined the Brigade from the 33rd. D.A.C., and was posted to A/156.	
			Lieut. T. P. Lysaght, A/156, was posted to the 33rd. D.A.C.	
	28/6/17		Major H. K. Saddler D.S.O. M.C. assumed temporary command of the Brigade, during the absence of Lieut. Col. B. A. B. Butler.	

CASUALTIES.

	Killed.	Wounded.
Officers.	NIL.	NIL.
Other Ranks.	NIL.	8.

H K Saddler
Major R.F.A.
Commanding 156th. Brigade R.F.A.

2353 Wt. W2544/1454 700,000 5/15 D. D. & L. A.D.S.S./Forms/C. 2118.

(1) 156th Brigade R.F.A.

Instructions regarding War Diaries and Intelligence Summaries are contained in F. S. Regs., Part II. and the Staff Manual respectively. Title pages will be prepared in manuscript.

WAR DIARY
or
INTELLIGENCE SUMMARY.

(Erase heading not required.)

June 1917

Vol 17

Army Form C. 2118.

Place	Date	Hour	Summary of Events and Information	Remarks and references to Appendices
In the field In the field FEUCHY.	5/6/17		The Brigade assisted in support of an attack by the 9th. Division, to capture and consolidate a line of shell-holes on Greenland Hill. For 5 days previous to this, a series of Chinese Barrages had been carried out on this target, and at 8pm. on the 5th. the Infantry attacked, and obtained the objective with very little resistance.	
	7/6/17		From this date until the 14th., a systematic destructive bombardment was carried out daily, in order to obliterate the enemy's defences and to weaken his morale.	
	10/6/17		The VIIth.Corps took over part of the line South of the River Scarpe, and thus the 9th. Division was astride the river.	
	14/6/17		The 76th. Infantry Brigade attacked HOOK TRENCH and LONG TRENCH, in order to establish themselves on the commanding ground on INFANTRY HILL. During the previous week's bombardment, there had been no firing Between 5am. and 9am. daily. At 7-20am. the Infantry rushed over and got into the enemy'strench, the artillery barrage not starting until 7-21½am. The attack took the enemy by surprise, and all o obje ctives gained, 30 prisoners and 2 Machine Guns being captured.	APPENDIX I.
	20/6/17		The Brigade withdrew to wagon-lines.	
	21/6/17		[illegible]	

#353 Wt. W2544/1454 700,000 5/15 D. D. & L. A.D.S.S./Forms/C. 2118.

(2) 155th Brigade RFA.

Instructions regarding War Diaries and Intelligence Summaries are contained in F. S. Regs., Part II. and the Staff Manual respectively. Title pages will be prepared in manuscript.

WAR DIARY
or
INTELLIGENCE SUMMARY.
(Erase heading not required.)

June 1917 (contd).

Army Form C. 2118.

Place	Date	Hour	Summary of Events and Information	Remarks and references to Appendices
In the field. HENIN.	21/6/17		The Brigade moved from the VIth. Corps area into the VIIth. Corps area. and relieved the I23rd. Brigade R.F.A. of the 37th. Divisional Artillery. Positions of Batteries- Headquarters. T.32.d.3.6. A. Battery. T.4.d.8.9. B. Battery. T.IO.b.2,8. C, Battery. T.4.d.6.4. D. Battery. T.4.a.O.5.	
	24/6/17		The Brigade, being now in support of the 33rd. Divisional Infantry, supported an attack by the I9th. Infantry Brigade, on Tunnel Trench from Lump Lane. This attack was unsuccessful.	
	26/6/17	I2 Mdt.	B Battery assisted in support of an attack by the 50th. Division on a line U.I.b.8.O. - U.I.b.9.7.. This attack was successful, but later the enemy regained all the ground captured.	
	29/6/17		At II-50am. the IOOth. Infantry Brigade carried out a raid on the portion of Tunnel Trench occupiedby the enemy immediately South of the CROISILLES - FONTAINE Road. The Brigade supported this raid. This raid was unsuccessful.	

2353 Wt. W2544/1454 700,000 5/15 D. D. & L. A.D.S.S./Forms/C. 2118.

APPENDIX I.

33rd D.A.
S.C. 782.

33rd Divisional Artillery.

It is with great pleasure that I forward the attached letter from the G.O.C. 3rd Division. I have already written to you to express my personal thanks to the Artillery supporting the Division.

Sd. J.S. OLLIVANT, Brig. General, R.A.,
20.6.17. Commanding R.A. 3rd Division.

2.

O.C. 156th Brigade, R.F.A.
,, 162nd ,,

The General Officer Commanding 33rd Division has expressed his gratification at this report.

I am much pleased that the batteries have so well maintained their reputation for straight shooting and effective co-operation with the Infantry.

C. Stewart

Brigadier General, R.A.,
26.6.17. Commanding 33rd Divisional Artillery.

C.R.A.,

3rd Division.

Will you please convey to all the artillery under your command the thanks and appreciation of all in the 3rd Division for tho splendid co-operation and assistance given during the operations 14th - 19th June, 1917.

The large share in our success which is attributable to all our supporting batteries is fully realized. Their constant protection and immediato readiness was invaluable, and we should be glad if every officer and man could be assured how much his individual efforts have contributed to the important success gained, and to the severe loss which must have been inflicted on the enemy.

We wish them all good fortune in the future and hope that we may again fight together with that close co-operation which has been so conspicuously marked whilst we have been together.

C. J. Deverell

Major-General,
Commanding 3rd Division.

19th June, 1917.

JULY 1917.

156th Brigade R.F.A.

Army Form C. 2118.

WAR DIARY
or
INTELLIGENCE SUMMARY.
(Erase heading not required.)

Instructions regarding War Diaries and Intelligence Summaries are contained in F. S. Regs., Part II. and the Staff Manual respectively. Title pages will be prepared in manuscript.

Vol 18

Place	Date	Hour	Summary of Events and Information	Remarks and references to Appendices
	1			
	1st		Alternative positions chosen by all Batteries.	
	2nd		New S.O.S. lines registered by Batteries.	
			Brigade zone - U.7 d.7.7. to U.1 d.5.5. Sheet 51b S.W.	
			A/156 considerably "crumped". 3 Sergeants killed.	
	3/4	night.	A/156 move one section to new position.	
	4th		2/Lieut.C.P.HENZELL and 2/Lieut A.A.BRUCE joined and posted to A and B Batteries respectively.	
	4/5	,,	A/156 move second section to new position.	
	5th		Registration completed by A/156.	
	7th		New S.O.S. lines registered by batteries.	
			Bde zone - U.13 b.60.95 - U.7 d.80.10 - U.7 b.50.00. Sheet 51b S.W.	
	8/9	,,	Night firing on selected "sore" points.	
	10/11	,,	1 Section per 18pr Bty and 2 sections per 4.5" How Bty relieved by 51st Bde.	
	11/12	,,	Relief by 51st Bde R.F.A. completed.	
			156th Bde R.F.A. at rest in Wagon Lines at BOIRY ST RICHTRUDE.	
	13th		Divisional Scheme under C.R.A.	
	15th		Divisional Scheme under C,R,A,	
	18th		Divisional Artillery Horse Show.	
	22nd		Divisional Artillery Sports.	
	23rd		Brigade marched and billetted at AMPLIER.	
	24/25		Brigade marched and entrained at DOULLENS SOUTH for ADINKERQUE and DUNKERQUE.	
	25/26		Marched from detraining stations to wagon lines at COXYDE BAINS.	
	28/29		Remainder of Brigade went into action.	
	29/28 30th		Brigade supporting 66th Division, between the coast & LOMBARDZYDE.	

B. Butler Lieut. Col.
Commanding 156th Brigade R.F.A.

2353 Wt. W2544/1454 700,000 5/15 D. D. & L. A.D.S.S./Forms/C. 2118.

August 1917.

156th Brigade R.F.A.

Instructions regarding War Diaries and Intelligence Summaries are contained in F. S. Regs., Part II. and the Staff Manual respectively. Title pages will be prepared in manuscript.

WAR DIARY
or
INTELLIGENCE SUMMARY.
(Erase heading not required.)

Army Form C. 2118.

Vol 19

Place	Date	Hour	Summary of Events and Information	Remarks and references to Appendices
COXYDE BAINS	1st.		Wagon Lines move back from COXYDE BAINS to LA PANNE.	
	2nd.		Assisted Infantry of 49th Division in a daylight raid.	
	5th		Wagon Lines moved forward from LA PANNE to COXYDE BAINS.	
	7/8	night	Assisted in two raids on Right Divisional Front, one on LOMBARTZYDE Sector, and one on the St GEORGES Sector. Both Raids were successful.	
	8/9	night	Fired in conjunction with launching of a projector Gas attack on the NIEUPORT BAINS Sector.	
	11th		2/Lieut.S.W.SWAINE, C/156 transferred to R.F.C.	
	14/15	night	B/156 withdrew to Wagon Lines for rest.	
	15/16	night	Projector Gas Attack on NIEUPORT BAINS Sector. Fired on GOLF Rd and POLDER Trench.	
	16th		Special destructive shoot by 4.5" Hows. on BARE Avenue. Lieut. & Adjutant, B.L.OXLEY wounded and evacuated. Six 18-pdr Batteries under Lt.Col.B.A.B.BUTLER of Left Div.Arty, transferred for S.O.S. purposes to Right Div. arty.	
	18th		Fired in practice barrage on Right Div. Front.	
	21st		Practice barrage on Right Div. Front. Fired on S.O.S. Lines.	
	22nd		Destructive shoot by 4.5" Hows. on POLDER Avenue. Fired in Practice barrage on Left Div. Front.	
	24/25	night	Infantry of 19th Infantry Brigade attacked and captured GELEIDE POST (M.22.d.1.5) 18-pdrs fired on S.O.S. lines. 6 prisoners and 1 Machine gun were captured.	
	25/26	night	GELEIDE POST recaptured by enemy, and our posts re-established on right bank of GELEIDE BROOK.	
	26/27	night	Projector Gas Attack on NIEUPORT BAINS Sector. Fired on area M.15.a.00.45 to a.00.00 - b.00.00 - 00.09.	
	27/28	night	156th Brigade R.F.A. withdrew from action without casualties to Wagon Lines at COXYDE BAINS.	
	29th		Lieut.W.G.SHEERES transferred from A/156 to H.Q/156 and appointed Adjutant, vice Lieut B.L.OXLEY wounded.	

August 1917.
156th Brigade R.F.A.

Instructions regarding War Diaries and Intelligence Summaries are contained in F. S. Regs., Part II. and the Staff Manual respectively. Title pages will be prepared in manuscript.

WAR DIARY
or
INTELLIGENCE SUMMARY.
(Erase heading not required.)

Army Form C. 2118.

Place	Date	Hour	Summary of Events and Information	Remarks and references to Appendices
COXYDE BAINS	29th		2/Lieut (A/Capt) BURRIDGE.C.E. transferred to 33rd D.A.C.	

CASUALTIES for MONTH

	KILLED	WOUNDED.
Officers.	NIL	1
Other Ranks.	8	13 (1 died of wounds)

C G G Spreres Capt adjt
for Lt.Col.R.F.A.
Commanding 156th Brigade R.F.A.

2353 Wt. W2544/1454 700,000 5/15 D. D. & L. A.D.S.S./Forms/C. 2118.

September 1917.

156th Brigade R.F.A.

Instructions regarding War Diaries and Intelligence Summaries are contained in F. S. Regs., Part II. and the Staff Manual respectively. Title pages will be prepared in manuscript.

WAR DIARY
or
INTELLIGENCE SUMMARY.
(Erase heading not required.)

Army Form C. 2118.

Original

33rd Divn

Vol 20

Place	Date	Hour	Summary of Events and Information	Remarks and references to Appendices
COXYDE BAINS	1st		Brigade in Wagon Lines at COXYDE BAINS.	
UXEM	2nd		Brigade left Coxyde and proceeded to UXEM.	
ZERMEZELLE.	3rd		Brigade left UXEM and proceeded to ZERMEZELLE.	
RENNINGHELST.	4th		Brigade left ZERMEZELLE and proceeded to RENNINGHELST.	
	5/6th		1 Section of "A", "B" & "C" Batteries went into action relieving sections of 11th, 12th and A/298 Batteries R.F.A. respectively.	
	6/7th		Another Section of "A", "B" & "C" Batteries went into action relieving sections of 11th, 12th and A/298 Batteries respectively.	
	7/8th		Another Section of "A", "B" & "C" Batteries went into action relieving sections of 11th, 12th and A"298 Batteries respectively.	
	10th		2/Lieut C.P.HENZELL, posted from A/156 to No. 2 Section 33rd D.A.C.	
	13th		Lt.Col.BUTLER, and H.Q/156 Bde R.F.A., relieved Lt.Col HAMILTON (21st D.A. "A" Group) and took over command of Right Group 23rd D.A., consisting of "A", "B", "C", & D/156, C/162, and D/315.	
	13/14th		Bombardment commenced.	
	15th		Corps Barrage, 4 p.m.	
	16th		Corps Barrage 5.30 a.m. Army Barrage 10 a.m.	
	17th		Corps Barrage. Zero Hour 3 p.m. 9th York and Lancs made a successful raid on German Post at J.20.a.32.42.	
	18th		Two Army Barrages. One at 6 a.m. and one at 8.30 p.m.	
	19th		2/Lieut R.T.LEIGH, B/156, wounded inaction. Corps Barrage 11 a.m.	
	20th		2/Lieut A.D.McEWAN and 2/Lieut H.E.PHIPPS, C/156, wounded in action. Second Army attacked on a front of about 8 miles Zero hour 5.40 a.m. Right Group supported 68th Inf.Bde, 23rd Division.	

2353 Wt. W2544/1454 700,000 5/15 D. D. & L. A.D.S.S./Forms/C. 2118.

Instructions regarding War Diaries and Intelligence Summaries are contained in F. S. Regs., Part II. and the Staff Manual respectively. Title pages will be prepared in manuscript.

WAR DIARY
or
INTELLIGENCE SUMMARY.
(Erase heading not required.)

Army Form C. 2118.

Place	Date	Hour	Summary of Events and Information	Remarks and references to Appendices
	20th Cont.		Final objective :- WARNETON LINE running through J.21.b & c.	
			Attack successful and 2/300 prisoners captured also 1 gun and 3 Howitzers.	
			Altough our right was in the air, several counter attacks were successfully repulsed during 20th/21st	
			Capt.BEERBOHM.C.E., B/156 attached to D/162.	
	22nd		Hostile Artillery exceedingly active.	
	23rd		2/Lieut F.W. BEADLE A/156, wounded in action.	
			Corps preparatory barrge at 7 a.m.	
	24th		Numerous Counter attacks on 33rd Divnl. Front. All successfully repulsed.	
			2/Lieut R.M.WINGFIELD B/156 wounded in action.	
			Group re-adjusted. Right Group consisting of "A" &B/156 C/162, A/103, "B", "C" & "D"/242. "C" &D/156 under command of Centre Group (Lt.Col.COCKCRAFT).	
	25th		Second Army continued their attacks. Zero hour 5.50am. 33rd Division attacked and after very severe fighting were everywhere successful.	
			2/Lieut B.SALL, B/156 wounded in action.	
	26th		Enemy counter attacked in force but were again successfully repulsed. Capt.C.E.BEERBOHM B/156 killed.	
			2/Lieut HOLMES, attached to B/156 from /33 T.M.Bty.	
	27th		Fired in Army Barrage 5 a.m.	
	28th		Army Barrage 5.20 a.m.	
			Group re-adjusted. Right Group consisting of "A","B" "C" & D/156 A/103 and C/162.	
	28/29th		Fairly heavy gas bombardment of Battery areas.	
	29th		Barrage 5.15 a.m.	
	30th		2/Lieut C.A.BLOOR, A/156 wounded in action. 2/Lieut MOUSLEY C/162 Bde ~~killed~~ WOUNDED in action.	

[signature] 2/Lt for Lt.Col.
Commanding 156th Brigade R.F.A.

TOTAL CASUALTIES FOR MONTH

	KILLED	WOUNDED.
OFFICERS	1	4
Other Ranks.	14	66

8353 Wt. W2544/1454 700,000 5/15 D. D. & L. A.D.S.S./Forms/C. 2118.

October 1917. 11

WAR DIARY
or
INTELLIGENCE SUMMARY.
(Erase heading not required.)

Army Form C. 2118.

156 F.A Bde

Vol 21

Instructions regarding War Diaries and Intelligence Summaries are contained in F. S. Regs., Part II. and the Staff Manual respectively. Title pages will be prepared in manuscript.

Place	Date	Hour	Summary of Events and Information	Remarks and references to Appendices
Near ZILLEBEKE	1st		2/Lieut P.R.M.HANNA, wounded.	
			Fired in two Army Practice Barrages.	
	2nd		2/Lieut C.J.L.LUTYENS, died of wounds.	
			Fired in Army Practice Barrages.	
	3rd		Enemy penetrated Right Battalion front in the morning but were counter attacked and driven out. A second enemy attack successfully repulsed. Line as before.	
		3 pm.	Fired in Army Practice Barrage.	
			2/Lieut E.R.WHEATLY posted to C/156.	
			2/Lieut WHEATLY died of wounds.	
	4th	6 am	Second Army attacked on a front of about 11,000 yards. This attack apparently coincided with a hostle attack prepared with 3 Divisions, partly on Xth Corps and partly on front of the Corps on our left. The hostile attack was broken up by our barrage at Zero. Penetrated the enemy's defences to a maximum depth of about 1,4000 yards and all final objectives taken, i.e. BITTER WOOD - BERRY COTTS - N. part of GHELUVELT WOOD - REUTEL VILLAGE- NOORDENHOEK VILLAGE - thence northwards to 100 yards West of Cross Roads at NIEUWEMOLEN and N.W. to KRONPINZ FARM including ABRAHAM HEIGHTS and GRAVENSTAFEL Village.	
			Enemy's casualties reported to be heavy.	
			Supported Right Battalion Right Infantry Brigade.	
			Capt.S.TALBOT, A/156 to Hospital.	
	5th		2/Lieut L.McLEOD, Posted to C/156.	
			2/Lieut L.HARKNETT, posted to B/156.	
	6th		2/Lieut W.M.B.NEWCOMB, posted to B/156.	
	9th		Second Army attacked. Supported Right Battalion Right Infantry Brigade.	
			2/Lieut E.B.LAWSON, posted to A/156.	
	10th		2/Lieut J.A.McCHALLIS, and 2/Lieut C.H.GOODERHAM posted to C/156.	

2353 Wt. W2544/1454 700,000 5/15 D. D. & L. A.D.S.S./Forms/C. 2118.

:October 1917.

Instructions regarding War Diaries and Intelligence Summaries are contained in F. S. Regs., Part II. and the Staff Manual respectively. Title pages will be prepared in manuscript.

WAR DIARY
or
INTELLIGENCE SUMMARY.

(Erase heading not required.)

Army Form C. 2118.

Place	Date	Hour	Summary of Events and Information	Remarks and references to Appendices
Near ZILLEBEKE	10th (cont).		2/Lieut W.C.MORGAN to Hospital.	
			2/Lieut C.H.CLEGG posted to D/156.	
	13th		H.Q/156, relieved by 27th Brigade 5th Division.	
			A/156, personnel to Wagon Lines.	
	14th		C/156, personnel to Wagon Lines.	
	16th		2/Lieut A.A.KENNINGHAM posted to A/156.	
	17th		A/156 returned to Action.	
			B/156, personnel to Wagon Lines.	
	18th		C/156 returned to Action.	
			D/156 personnel to Wagon Lines.	
	19th		2/Lieut L.PESKIN, posted to B/156.	
	22nd		2/Lieut S.W.WILLETT, C/156, wounded in action.	
	23rd		2/Lieut H.B.MOLYNEUX, B/156, to Hospital (gas poisoning).	
	26th		Second Army attacked. Supported Right Battalion Right Infantry Brigade.	
			2/Lieut W.R.F.FISHER, posted to A/156.	
	28th		2/Lieut H.DUNCAN, posted to D/156.	
			"A" and C/156 pulled out and proceed to Wagon Lines.	
	29th		D/156, heavily shelled with H.E. and gas.	
			Major W.A.T.BARSTOW and 2/Lieut D.H.REVELS to Hospital (gas poisoning).	
	31st		D/156, pulled out and proceeded to Wagon Line.	

TOTAL CASUALTIE FOR MONTH.

	OFFICERS	OTHER RANKS
Killed		10
Wounded (includes Gassed).	7	128

B. Butler. Lt.Col.R.F.A.
Commanding 156th Brigade R.F.A.

2353 Wt. W2544/1454 700,000 5/15 D. D. & L. A.D.S.S./Forms/C. 2118.

NOVEMBER 1917.

16

Instructions regarding War Diaries and Intelligence Summaries are contained in F. S. Regs., Part II. and the Staff Manual respectively. Title pages will be prepared in manuscript.

WAR DIARY
or
INTELLIGENCE SUMMARY.
(Erase heading not required.)

Army Form C. 2118.

156 Bde R.F.A.

Vol 22

Place	Date	Hour	Summary of Events and Information	Remarks and references to Appendices
	2nd		B/156 pulled out of action.	
			2/Lieut.E.B.LAWSON admitted to Hospital.	
	3rd		2/Lt.C.R.HERSCHEL posted to B/156.	
	4th.		Brigade marched to billets at LE NIEPPE.	
	6th		2/Lt.A.J MINSON posted to D/156.	
	7th.		2/Lt K.R.BLACKWELL posted to A/156.	
	8th		2/Lt O.CLOW posted to C/156.	
	11th		Major D.E.Jones posted to command D/156.	
	12th		Brigade marched to billets in BOUVELINCHEM area. Headquarters, "A" & "C" Batteries billeted at JOURNY, "B" Battery at BAS LOQUIN, and "D" Battery at WARLEZ.	
	14th		2/Lt H.DUNCAN, posted to D/246 Brigade R.F.A.	
	23rd		2/Lt J.T.GORMAN to School of Signalling at DUNSTABLE.	
			2/Lt G.W.WILLIAMSON posted to C/156.	
Casualties for month NIL.			Commanding 156th Brigade R.F.A. [signature] Lt.Col.R.F.A.	

2353 Wt. W2544/1454 700,000 5/15 D. D. & L. A.D.S.S./Forms/C. 2118.

DECEMBER 1917. 156th Brigade R.F.A. 6

Army Form C. 2118.

Instructions regarding War Diaries and Intelligence Summaries are contained in F. S. Regs., Part II. and the Staff Manual respectively. Title pages will be prepared in manuscript.

WAR DIARY
or
INTELLIGENCE SUMMARY.
(Erase heading not required.)

Original
156 Bde R.F.A.
Vol 23

Place	Date	Hour	Summary of Events and Information	Remarks and references to Appendices
	2nd		Brigade marched to and billeted in ZERMEZEELE Area.	
	3rd		Brigade marched to and occupied wagon lines 1½ miles E. of VLAMERTINGHE.	
	4th		A, B & C/156 batteries into action N. of ZONNEBEKE.	
	7th.		H.Q/156 relieved H.Q./158 A.F.A.Bde. Lt-Col.BUTLER took over command of No.1 Group, consisting of:- A,B & C/156 and A,B,C & D/162. Capt.O.E.GALLIE D.S.O.,M.C., killed in action. 2/Lt.A.R.MacDONALD A/156 wounded in action.	
	9th		2/Lt E.B.LAWSON A/156 rejoined from Hospital.	
	12th		No.1 Group re-organised; A,B,C & D/162 to No.2 Group. No.1 Group consisted of A,B,C & D/156 and D/186.	
	16th		2/Lt. D. McLEOD C/156 wounded in action.	
	17th		Major F.B.H.CARRELL provisionally posted and attached to C/156.	
	18th		2/Lt. J.GREIG posted to D/156.	
	24th		B/250 from No.3 Group to No.1 Group to replace D/186. Major.H.McA.RICHARDS to Hospital sick. Capt.E.H.PRIOR and Lt.L.VESTEY struck off strength. (M.B. in England)	
	26th.		One section each Battery (personnel) withdrew to W.L.	
	27th		Remainder of Batteries and H.Q./156 withdrew to wagon lines. Relieved by 48th Army Field Arty. Bde.	
	29th.		2/Lt.A.L.DARBY posted to A/156.	
	31st		Capt.A.HEADS from Y/33 T.M.B. to 2nd in command D/156.	

H.W. Barnard 2/Lt
for. O.C. 156 Bde RFA
1/1/18.

2353 Wt. W2544/1454 700,000 5/15 D. D. & L. A.D.S.S./Forms/C. 2118.

JANUARY 1918. 11 156th Brigade R.F.A.,

Instructions regarding War Diaries and Intelligence Summaries are contained in F. S. Regs., Part II. and the Staff Manual respectively. Title pages will be prepared in manuscript.

WAR DIARY
or
INTELLIGENCE SUMMARY.
(Erase heading not required.)

Army Form C. 2118.

156 Bde RFA
Vol 24

Place	Date	Hour	Summary of Events and Information	Remarks and references to Appendices
	1st		Capt. F.C.PACKHAM posted to A/156 from 33rd D.A.C.	
			Major F.B.H.CARRELL joined from Base and posted to 156th Bde with effect from 1.1.18.	
	7/8th		Brigade relieved 250th Bde R.F.A. and Lt.Col B.A.B.BUTLER DSO took over command of No.1 Group, consisting of A,B,C & D/156 and B/119.	
	11th		2/Lt.F.E.S.GROVES posted to C/156.	
	17th		Lt.Col B.A.B.BUTLER DSO proceeded to England to attend Course at SALISBURY.	
			2/Lt.P.W.COLLEY joined and posted to A/156.	
			2/Lt.G.E.WILSON joined and posted to B/156.	
	22nd		2/Lt.R.E.W.McDONALD joined and posted to C/156.	
	27th		2/Lt.A.L.DARBY A/156 attached to Trench Mortars 33rd D.A.,	
	29th/30th		~~Maxxx~~ Batteries relieved by 250th Bde R.F.A.,	
	30th		Command of No.1 Group handed over to 250th Bde R.F.A.,	
			156th Brigade R.F.A. marched and billetted at OUDEZEELE.	
			Major N.G.M.JERVIS posted to command A/156 and temporarily command 156th Bde R.F.A. during absence of Lt-Col.B.A.B.BUTLER D.S.O., attending course.	
	31st.		Brigade marched and billetted at ZUDROVE.	

H W Bonnail Offr for Maj.
Cmdg 156 Bde RFA.

2353 Wt. W2544/1454 700,000 5/15 D. D. & L. A.D.S.S./Forms/C. 2118.

FEBRUARY 1918.

156th Brigade R.F.A.,

Army Form C. 2118.

156 Bde RFA

Vol 25

WAR DIARY
or
INTELLIGENCE SUMMARY.

(*Erase heading not required.*)

Instructions regarding War Diaries and Intelligence Summaries are contained in F. S. Regs., Part II. and the Staff Manual respectively. Title pages will be prepared in manuscript.

Place	Date	Hour	Summary of Events and Information	Remarks and references to Appendices
	1st		Brigade marched to and billetted at THIEMBRONNE.	
	9th		2/Lt.H.A.FOWLE joined and posted to A/156.	
	11th) 12th)		A,B & C Batteries to TILQUES for calibration.	
	13th		A,B & C Batteries attached to 98th Infantry Brigade for Tactical Exercise in TILQUES Area.	
			2/Lt.W.H.ORCHARD joined and posted to B/156.	
	16th		B/156 to TILQUES for re-calibration.	
			2/Lt.A.L.DARBY A/156 posted to Y/33 T.M.Bty.	
			2/Lt.B.HARKNETT B/156 posted to 33rd D.A.C.	
	18th		Lt-Col.B.A.B.BUTLER D.S.O. returned from Course in England.	
	19th		Brigade marched to and billetted at ELNES.	
	20th		Brigade marched to and billetted at LE NIEPPE.	
	21st		Brigade marched to and billetted at ZERMEZEELE.	
	22nd		Brigade marched to Wagon Lines; A,C & D at VLAMERTINGHE, B/156 at ASYLUM, YPRES.	
			One section A,B,C & D/156 relieved sections of A/250, B/251, A/251 & D/251 respectively.	
	23rd		Remainder of Batteries relieved remaining sections of A/250, B,A & D/251.	
			156th Bde.H.Q. relieved H.Q./251; Lt-Col.B.A.B.BUTLER D.S.O. taking over command of No.2 Group.	
			Lt.E.GILDON posted from 162nd Bde R.F.A. to D/156.	
	21st		2/Lt.T.F.JEFFERY joined.to 156th Brigade R.F.A.	

B. Butler Lt Col.
Cdg. 156 Bde R.F.A.

MARCH 1918. 156th Brigade R.F.A.,

Instructions regarding War Diaries and Intelligence Summaries are contained in F. S. Regs., Part II. and the Staff Manual respectively. Title pages will be prepared in manuscript.

WAR DIARY
or
~~INTELLIGENCE SUMMARY.~~
(Erase heading not required.)

Army Form C. 2118.

Original
156 Bde R.F.A.
Vol 26

Place	Date	Hour	Summary of Events and Information	Remarks and references to Appendices
Near ZONNEBEKE.	1st		Lieut.V.H.MILLER (Royal Horse Guards) attached 156th Bde as Adviser in Horsemastership.	
	13th		2/Lt.E.B.LAWSON B/156 wounded in action.	
	14th		Major.N.G.H.JERVIS attached to H.Q. 33rd D.A. and taken off strength of 156th Bde. R.F.A.,	
	21st) 22nd)	night of.	Fired in support of raid by 19th Infantry Bde, on the GASOMETERS. Raid was successful, but GASOMETERS found to be unoccupied.	
	22nd		2/Lt. C.R.HERSCHELL B/156 posted to Fifth Army. 2/Lt.H.E.PHIPPS rejoined and posted to C/156.	
	27th		Capt (A/Major) F.B.H.CARRELL A/156 posted to 6th Div.	
	28th) 29th)		1 Section each of B, C & D/156 moved to alternate positions at D.14 c.9.6., D.27 a.35.75, and D.14 a.7.3. respectively.	
	29th) 30th)		1 Section each of B, C & D/156 moved to alternate positions at D.14 c.9.6., D.27 a.35.75., and D.14 a.7.3. respectively. (Ref:- Map Sheet ZONNEBEKE 28 N.E.1 1/10,000.)	

31/3/18.

H.W. Burnell
Capt for Lt Col
Cmdg 156 Bde R.F.A.

2353 Wt. W2544/1454 700,000 5/15 D. D. & L. A.D.S.S./Forms/C. 2118.

33rd Divisional Artillery.

156th BRIGADE R.F.A. ::: APRIL 1918.

April 1918 — 156th Brigade R.F.A. — Original — Vol 27

Instructions regarding War Diaries and Intelligence Summaries are contained in F. S. Regs., Part II. and the Staff Manual respectively. Title pages will be prepared in manuscript.

Army Form C. 2118.

WAR DIARY
or
INTELLIGENCE SUMMARY.
(Erase heading not required.)

Place	Date	Hour	Summary of Events and Information	Remarks and references to Appendices
Near ZONNEBEKE	7th/8th		Brigade in action near ZONNEBEKE. Relieved by 28th Army Field Artillery Brigade (Col. PAYNTER) and proceeded to Wagon lines near VLAMERTINGHE.	
	10th	5pm	Left Wagon Lines, and marched to Wagon Lines near DRANOUTRE. Now under orders from CRA 25th Division	
	11th	3am	Left DRANOUTRE and marched to HALLEBAST CORNER. Wagon Lines established near LA CLYTTE. Batteries in action near VIERSTRAAT. Headquarters at PARRETT CAMP (Sheet 28 SW.)	
	12th		Headquarters "A" and "D" Batteries shelled.	
	13th		Headquarters moved to N.9.d.9.8 (Sheet 28 SW)	
	16th	5am	Raid by 62nd Infantry Brigade on cutting in N.30.d.88. 156 Brigade fired Box Barrage in support of same. Raid unsuccessful. 2/Lt JEFFREY wounded, and died of wounds same day.	
		6am	Hostile attack, after heavy barrage, took WYTSCHAETE and WYTSCHAETE WOOD.	
	17th	7.30pm	Fired in support of counter-attack on WYTSCHAETE. Attack unsuccessful.	
	18th		"C" Battery shelled. Lt G.W. WILLIAMSON wounded.	
	23rd		"A" Battery heavily shelled.	
	25th	2.30am–6am	Heavy barrage of HE and gas put down on front and support lines, Battery areas and lines of communication. About 6.10am enemy attacked on line VIERSTRAAT – KEMMEL Road. About 9am enemy had advanced to CHEAPSIDE LINE. Forward section of A/156 and detached Gun of D/156 surrounded and captured. Owing to heavy fire, only three Guns were got out. Remainder withdrawn from front line at dusk.	
			Lieut W.G. BRUCE, Brigade Signal Officer Killed. 2/Lt K.R. BLACKWELL, A/156 and 2/Lt O.W. CLOW, C/156 missing. Major A. BARKER, C/156, 2/Lt E.E.S. GROVES C/156, 2/Lt H.E. PHIPPS C/156, wounded.	
	26th		156th Brigade in action near MILLEKRUISSE. Lt L VESTEY posted to C/156.	
	27th		2/Lt J.G. GREIG, D/156 wounded remaining at duty.	
	28th		2/Lt D.H. REVELS posted to D/156. Brigade withdrawn to Wagon Lines	
	29th		Brigade marched to rest area near WINNEZEELE.	
	30th		2/Lt EASTWOOD R.E. posted to 156 Brigade.	

[signature] Capt for Lt Col
Commanding 156th Brigade RFA

2353 Wt. W2544/1454 700,000 8/15 D. D. & L. A.D.S.S./Forms/C. 2118.

Original

Army Form C. 2118.

May 1918

Instructions regarding War Diaries and Intelligence Summaries are contained in F. S. Regs., Part II. and the Staff Manual respectively. Title pages will be prepared in manuscript.

WAR DIARY
or
INTELLIGENCE SUMMARY.
(Erase heading not required.)

156th Brigade R.F.A.

No C28

Place	Date	Hour	Summary of Events and Information	Remarks and references to Appendices
WINNEZEELE.	1st		The Brigade in Second Army reserve at WINNEZEELE	
NR BRANDHOEK	8th		Relieved the 149th Brigade R.F.A. in action near BRANDHOEK.	
	11th		Lieut. K.W. MILNES joined and posted to A/156. 2/Lt. H.V. CUSHING joined and posted to C/156.	
	12th		Brigade withdrew to Wagon Lines. Front taken over by the French	
	13th		2/Lt. J. GREIG admitted to hospital, suffering from wounds received in action on 27/4/18.	
Clifford Camp	15th		Brigade marched and Billetted in Clifford Rest Camp (F.19 d 35 Sheet 27) near PROVEN, and in Tenth Corps reserve.	
			Lieut. T.Q. HARVEY transferred to R.A.F. 2/Lt. R.E.W. McDONALD transferred to 33rd D.A.C.	
	17th		2/Lieut. W.M.B. NEWCOMBE B/156 admitted to hospital.	
	18th		Lieut. E. MORRIS joined and posted to B/156. 2/Lt. R.E.N. BRADEN joined and posted to C/156. 2/Lieut. C.A.I. MOON joined and posted to D/156.	
	20th		33rd Division inspected by General PLUMER Commanding Second Army. Brigade represented by 4 Officers and 30 other ranks.	
	23rd		2/Lieut. H.H.B. PEARSON joined and posted to B/156. 2/Lieut. J. CORRIE joined & posted to D/156	
	27th		Capt. R.D. RUSSELL joined and posted to C/156. 2/Lt. C.J. FULLER joined and posted to A/156. 2/Lieut. W.H. SNELL joined and posted to B/156. 2/Lieut. E.J. WHITE joined & posted to D/156.	

(A9175) Wt W2358/P360 600,000 12/17 D. D. & L. Sch. 52a. Forms/C2118/15

H.M. Bonar? Lt Col
Commanding 156 Brigade RFA

JUNE 1918

Confl 33

WAR DIARY of 156th Brigade R.F.A. or ~~INTELLIGENCE SUMMARY.~~

(Erase heading not required.)

Army Form C. 2118.

Vol 29

Instructions regarding War Diaries and Intelligence Summaries are contained in F. S. Regs., Part II, and the Staff Manual respectively. Title pages will be prepared in manuscript.

Place	Date	Hour	Summary of Events and Information	Remarks and references to Appendices
	1st		156 Bde RFA in Corps Res, stationed at CLIFFORD CAMP 27/F 19 D	
	1st/2nd		One section each of A.B.C.D/156 relieve one section each of A.B.C.D/245 in action in the CANAL SECTOR	
	2/3		Relief completed. Batteries at H16c H15c, H22A and H10A (Sheet 28 NW).	
			Brigade in support of 71st I.B and covering zone I 32A 80.50 – I 32A 62.95	
	5th		1.15 a.m. D/156 fired in support of raid by 9th Leicesters on trench I 32A 30.42 – 60.50. Raid not successful.	
			11.15 pm 156 Bde. fired in support of raid on enemy posts in LANKHOF FARM. Raiding party was composed of men of the 2nd York & Lancasters. Barrage good but raid unsuccessful.	
	7/8		71st I.B (6th Div) relieved by 100 I.B (33rd Div)	
	8th		4.37 am. 46th French Regt supported by its own Artillery plus Artillery of 156 and 162 Bde. RFA attacked RIDGE WOOD and SCOTTISH WOOD. Attack completely successful between 60 and 70 prisoners being taken. About 12 noon a hostile counter attack left RIDGE WOOD in the hands of the enemy.	
	9th		Brigade H.Q moved to H 22 A 2.7.	
	13th		3.51 a.m French (46th Regt) again attacked RIDGE WOOD. Attack successful and 47 prisoners taken. 156 Bde. assisted by barraging along the ELZENVALLE – BRASSERIE Road. Later in the day a hostile counter attack succeeded in regaining RIDGE WOOD	
			CAPT. AULTON A.V.C. posted to the Brigade.	
	14th		2/LT J PICKEN, Glasgow Yeomanry attached as Horsemaster.	
	20th		12.15 a.m. 156 Bde. put down box barrage in support of raid by 1st Middlesex on trench I 32A 45.40 – I 32A 63.52. English covering party met a German covering party in 'No Mans Land' at Zero -3. Fighting followed and English covering party reinforced by raiding party drove enemy back into his trench. Fierce fighting followed but no identifications were obtained.	
	23rd		12.55 a.m. Gas successfully projected from I 26 B 2.8 and I 21c 1.5. Special harassing programme fired by 156 Brigade. R.F.A.	
	24th		2/Lt A.A. BRUCE killed in action	
	25th		Lt R. COOPER. M.C. and 2/Lt H.N.H. SPENCER joined the Brigade and posted to A and C Batteries respectively.	
	28th		3.10 a.m. Fired barrage in Chinese attack as counter attraction to attack near VIEUX BERQUIN.	
	30th		9.30 p.m. 11th A.F.A. Bde. RFA withdrawn from action.	
			156 Bde. RFA took over support of Left Inf. Bde. 33rd Div.	
			A.B & C/156 take over positions of 83rd 85th and D/11 Batteries respectively.	[signature] 30/6/18

JULY 1918

Instructions regarding War Diaries and Intelligence Summaries are contained in F. S. Regs., Part II, and the Staff Manual respectively. Title pages will be prepared in manuscript.

WAR DIARY of 156th Brigade R.F.A. or ~~INTELLIGENCE SUMMARY.~~

(*Erase heading not required.*)

Army Form C. 2118.

Vol 30

Place	Date	Hour	Summary of Events and Information	Remarks and references to Appendices
	1st.		156 Bde.R.F.A.in action in CANAL Sector in support of Left Inf.Bde.33rd Div	
	3rd.	12.5 a.m	Fired creeping barrage on areaLANKHOF FARM and CHATEAU to SPOIL BANK	
	4th	11 pm.	A & B/156 put down barrage along Southern Bank of ZILLEBEKE LAKE to assist in raid by 49th Div.on enemy posts in I.16 d. (Sheet 28 N.W).	
	6th	11.45 p.m.	A party of 9th H.L.I.raided enemy trench I.32.a.13.30 - 65.53. 156 Bde. assisted by putting down box barrage round area to be raided. Barrage good, but raid unsuccessful as raiders were caught by enemy barrage	
	7/8th		Artillery of 33rd D.A.reinforced by 186 Bde.R.F.A.(39th D.A). This resulted in reorganisation of Field Artillery Covering Div.Front.	
	8th	6 a.m	156 Bde.in support of Left Battn.Right Bde.covering front from YPRES COMINES Canal inclusive to VOORMEZEELE.	
	13th		2nd.Lt.TETLOW and 2nd Lt.MARTIN posted to 156 Bde.R.F.A.	
	14th	12.25 a.m	5th Scottish Rifles raided Farm I 27.c.57.55 (Sheet 28 N.W) 2Btys. 156 Bde. assisted in barrage. D/156 bombarded M.Gs.in LANKHOF FARM and CHATEAU.	
		6.a.m	18th L.B. (6th Div) and 1 Coy.33rd.Div.made an attack to regain old front line N.5.c.7.9. - b.12.08. - b.80.77 - H.36.b.45.30. All guns 156 Bde. fired in barrage. Attack was completely successful,all objectives were gained and a total of 7 Offs. and 313 O.Rs.captured. During the day enemy T.Ms. and M.Gs.successfully engaged and knocked out.	
		11.30 a.m.	Enemy reported dribbling up in small parties - and one large party - presumably for counter-attack. Concentration on VOORMEZEELE and VOORMEZEELE - St.ELOI ROAD were put down and enemy scattered in all directions.	
		12.30 p.m.	2nd Lt.TETLOW wounded. During remainder of day 156 Bde.put down several concentrations. Harassing fire and Counter Preparation kept up till dawn.	
	15th		All quiet.	
	17/18	Night	Fired Counter Preparation and concentrations as enemy attack was expected.	
	18/19	Night	Fired Counter Preparation.	
	20th		Lt-Col.B.A.B.BUTLER,D.S.O on leave to England. Major A.BARKER,D.S.O.,M.C, assumes temporary command of the Brigade.	
	28th		Major F.B.H.CARRELL on leave to England.	
	29th.		Batteries inspected by Brig.-Gen. G.H.W.NICHOLSON, C.M.G. Brig.-Gen. C.G.STEWART, C.M.G.,D.S.O proceeded to England on tour of duty at home. Brig.Gen.G.H.W.NICHOLSON, C.M.G assumes command of 33rd Div.Arty.	A. Barker Major R.F.A. Cmdg 156 Bde R.F.A.

31/7/18.

(A9173) Wt W2358/P360 600,000 12/17 D. D. & L. Sch. 52a. Forms/C2118/15

August 1918

Instructions regarding War Diaries and Intelligence Summaries are contained in F. S. Regs., Part II. and the Staff Manual respectively. Title pages will be prepared in manuscript.

WAR DIARY
or
INTELLIGENCE SUMMARY.
(Erase heading not required.)

Original

Army Form C. 2118.

156 Bde R.F.A.

VIII 31

Place	Date	Hour	Summary of Events and Information	Remarks and references to Appendices
	1st		156 Bde in action in CANAL SECTOR in support of Left Inf. Bde 33rd Div	
	3rd		156 Bde front altered. Bde now to cover Right Inf Bde	
			~~Operation Order No 15 issued~~	~~Appendix~~
	5th		Lt-Col. Butler DSO. returned from leave in England	
	7th		Major A. Barker DSO to Senior Officers course in England	
	10th		Capt. G.R. WESTFELDT of 113 American F.A. attached to H.Q 156 Bde	
	12th		48 hour visits of Infantry Officers to Batteries commenced.	
	13th		T/Major W. G SHEERES, M.C on leave to England	
	14th		Forward wagon lines brigaded at VLAMERTINGHE	
			Capt. G.R WESTFELDT A.F.A rejoined his unit.	
	17th		R.S.M. WOODWARD and 1 O.R per Battery proceeded for tour of duty at home under A.G.G.H.Q. letter CR.No 101900/A/c.	
	18th		33rd Divl Inf. relieved by Inf. of 30th American Div.	
			B.S.M. BAUDAINS appointed Act. R.S.M. vice R.S.M. WOODWARD	
	22nd		T/Capt W. G. PRINGLE, M.C posted to 156 Bde.	
			48 hour visits of Inf Officers to Batteries recommence.	
	26th		Bde School of Battery Staff work opened at Wagon Lines under Capt W. G PRINGLE M.C	
			A/Capt. A.C PACKHAM admitted to Hospital	
	28th		Concentration of F.A and T.M.s on VOORMEZEELE.	
			T/Major W. G. SHEERES returned from leave in England	
	29th		A/Capt A HEADS, M.C. transferred to 162nd Bde	
	28/29		R 156 Bde. R.F.A relieved by 330th Bde. R.F.A.	
	29/30		Relief by 330th Bde R.F.A completed.	
			Bde. marched to billets in HAANDEKOTE area	
	30th		Bde billets inspected by Brig. Gen. G.H.W. NICHOLSON, C.M.G.	
			Warning order received. Bde to be ready to entrain 31 Aug/1 Sept for Third Army	

[signature] Capt. R.F.A.
Adj. 156 Brigade R.F.A.

(A9175) Wt W2358/P360 500,000 12/17 D. D. & L. Sch 52a. Forms/C2118/15

September 1918.

WAR DIARY

Army Form C.2118.

156 Bde RFA

Place.	Date.	Hour.	Summary of events and information.	Remarks and references to Appendices.
PROVEN	1st	6.45am.	156th Bde R.F.A. entrained at PROVEN, en route for Third Army.	
Petitxxxx Houvain		7.45 p.m.	Detrained at PETIT HOVAIN and marched to billetts at REBREUVIETTE where Bde was put in Army Reserve,.	
			2/LEXXXX 2/Lt CLEGG D/156 Bde R.F.A. transferred to C/156 Bde R.F.A.	
REBREUV-IETTE.	4th		Half Battery D/156 calibrated at Thrid Army Calibration Range.	
	5th		Two Guns each of "A", "B" & "C" Batteries calibrated. Divisional Artillery inspected by G.O.C. 33rd Division.	
	6th		Remaining guns of 156 Bde R.F.A. sent to Calibration Range. Tactical Scheme in conjunction with 19th Infantry Brigade in the LA SOUICH Area. One 18-pdr Battery and 3 Howitzers took part in this scheme.	
	7th		Advance guard scheme in conjunction with 5th Scottish Rifles. "B" & D/156 Bde took part.	
	10th		Brigade Staff parade in LASOUICH area	
		5.30pm.	"SHRAPNELS" Concert Party gave performance to Brigade at REBREUVIETTE.	
	11th		Divisional Scheme in skeleton order in the CANELTMONT, REBREUVE, REBREUVIETTE area.	
	14th	8 pm.	156th Brigade R.F.A. left REBREUVIETTE, and marched via BOUQUEMAISON, - DOULLENS - and MARIEUX to billetts in ACHEUX.	
	15th	6.30 pm.	Marched via ALBERT - LE SARS - THILLOY - andBEAULENCOURT to LE TRANSLOY.	
	16th		Positions reconnoitred near HEUDECOURT for support of attacks by 17th Division, Vth Corps on the GOUZEAUCOURT - PEIZERE Line.	
Near	16/17		All Guns of 156th Brigade R.F.A. in action.	
HEUDECOURT	18th	5.20am.	17th Division with 38th Division on Left and 21st Division on right attacked along whole Corps front. 17th Division after fierce fighting gained their final objectives and consolidated North and East of GAUCHE WOOD. During afternoon and evening Artillery engaged many moving targets and successfully silenced hostile Machine Guns and Trench Mortars. Two counter attackxs were also successfully dispersed.	
		9 pm.	Supported with creeping barrage attack by 17th Division pushing North GAUCHE WOOD to ST QUENTIN redoubt, and GREEN LANE. Attack partially successful and final line consolidated just North of QUENTIN REDOUBT.	
	21st	5.40am.	33rd Division with 38th Division on Right attacked to gain final objectives for operation on 18th September. 156th Brigade R.F.A. put down Chinese Barrage on left of 33rd Division to cover the attackers flanks.	
	23rd		Batteries and H.Qrs., 156th Brigade R.F.A., moved forward from HEUDECOURT positions to area W.18. & W.24.(near PEIZIERE).	
	24th	3 pm.	100th Infantry Brigade 33rd Division attacked with objectives MEUNIER TRENCH. LEITH WALK and CLOSTER ROAD 156th Bde R.F.A. assisted by barraging hostile M.G areas. Attack successful.	

Sheet 2.

156th Brigade R.F.A.

WAR DIARY.

Army Form C.2118

September 1918.

Place.	Date	Hour.	Summary of events and information.	Remarks and references to appendices.
	24th		Between 24th and 28th fierce hand to hand fighting took place in GLOSTER Road area. Ground changed hands many times.	
Near PIEZIERE.	29th	3.30am.	98th Infantry Brigade attacked VILLERS GUSLAIN, one company working round on N.W., one ~~through~~ up through centre and one on S.E. side. Each company was supported by one TANK. Rollong barrage put down over the village by 33rd Divisional Artillery. Attack was apparently successful 200 prisoners being taken, but later on, situation became obscure, and in the afternoon village again reported in hands of the enemy.	
		5.50am.	156th Brigade R.F.A. supported attack by 100th Infantry Brigade with objectives, PIGEON TRENCH X.17 & X.23. with posts on line EVE COPSE - CRAWFORD CRATER., attack met with little success, and by evening infantry were back in their old line.	
	30th		Patrols sent out along 100th Brigade front. Reported enemy retiring across CANAL. By evening 100th Brigade main line along PIGEON TRENCH X.17 & X.23 with patrols along CANAL between HONNECOURT and OSSUS.	
		11am-2 pm.	Headquarters and Batteries of 156th Brigade R.F.A. moved forward to positions in X.26 & X.27.	

[signature] Lt-Col R.F.A.
Commanding 156th Brigade R.F.A.

156th Brigade R.F.A. 4

October 1918.

Instructions regarding War Diaries and Intelligence Summaries are contained in F. S. Regs., Part II. and the Staff Manual respectively. Title pages will be prepared in manuscript.

WAR DIARY
or
INTELLIGENCE SUMMARY.
(Erase heading not required.)

156 Bde RFA Vol 33

Army Form C. 2118. 33

Place	Date	Hour	Summary of Events and Information	Remarks and references to Appendices
OSSUS	1st		156th Bde R.F.A. in support of 100th Infantry Brigade in PIGEON TRENCH line near OSSUS. Batteries in action as under :- H.Q. X.22.c.6.6 A/156 X.21.d.20.10. B/156 X.16.c.15.10. C/156 X.16.d.65.30. D/156 X.21.c.65.20. X.22.c.40.40.	
	2nd		1 Section B/156 in action in PIGEON QUARRY.	
	2nd/3rd		100th Inf. Bde relieved by 5th Scottish Rifles.	
	3rd		No.632 Bdr WALKER, B/156 awarded Military Medal. Fired Gas concentration on LA TERRIERRE.	
	5th		At dawn 5thinst the 5th Scottish Rifles pushed patrols across River and with only slight resistance, advanced through FRANKUE WOOD and on through LA TERRIERE. At 15.00 Infantry had established themselves in AUBENCHEUL. By 4 p.m. 156th Brigade had made rough bridge over Canal St QUENTIN (S.7.d.00 approx) and at 5 pm A/156 and 1 section C/156 had taken up positions across Canal at S.21.a.55. and S.20.b central respectively. At dusk D/156 went into action at S.22.a.25.00, and 4 guns C/156 crossed the Canal and took up positions of readiness in S.20.b.	
	6th		At dawn 6th inst, remainder of Brigade crossed the Canal and at 10 a.m. Brigade was in action covering AUBENCHEUL as under :- H.Q/156 S.22.c.10.55. A/156 S.22.d.40.55. B/156 S.22.d.60.30. C/156 S.28.b.50.70. D/156 S.22.a.25.00.	
	8th	01.00	115th Inf.Bde. attacked with 2 Battalions, objective- BEAUREVOIR Line, and VILLERS OUTREUX and to road T.9.b - T.10.c. - T.16.b. After much opposition final objective was gained about 10.00 8th inst. At 10.10 156th Brigade R.F A. ordered forward to positions in T.19.a and b. to support an attack by 114th Inf. Bde. on MALINCOURT, with final objective road N.36.b & d, T.6.a, and U.1.c & d with posts at O.25. central and O.22.b.	

to sheet 2.

(A9175) Wt W2358/P360 650,000 12/17 D. D. & L. Sch 52a. Forms/C2118/15

WAR DIARY
or
INTELLIGENCE SUMMARY.
(Erase heading not required.)

Army Form C. 2118.

Instructions regarding War Diaries and Intelligence Summaries are contained in F. S. Regs., Part II, and the Staff Manual respectively. Title pages will be prepared in manuscript.

Place	Date	Hour	Summary of Events and Information	Remarks and references to Appendices
	8th		At 11.30 p.m. the Brigade was in action as under, and fired creeping barrage as ordered:- H.Q/156 S.18.d.7.2. A/156 T.19.a.3.8. B/156 T.19.a.25.50. C/156 T.19.a.90.50. D/156 T.19.a.30.30. At about noon, it was apparent that enemy was in full retreat, so barrage was stopped. Infantry pushed on with little opposition through MAILINCOURT, and about 15.00 hrs was on its final objective, but had not succeded in pushing out posts. At 2 p.m. 1 section of B/156, and shortly after 3 Howitzers D/156, were shooting in close support of Infantry and did excellent work engaging hostile movement, snipers and M.G's. By 4 p.m. 156th Bde R.F.A. was in action as under:- H.Q/156 T.10.c.10.40. A/156 T.11.d.10.40. B/156 T.11.c.20.90. C/156 T.10.b.70.05. D/156 T.10.d.60.35. and at 6 p.m. after continous successful sniping fired in support of an attack by 15th Welsh to gain high ground in O.32.b.	
	9th		At dawn 19th Infantry Brigade, 33rd Division pushed through 114th Infantry Brigade and continued the advance with little opposition ~~xx~~ as far as CLARY, but were held up in the village by snipers and M.G's. 2 Guns A/156 and 3 Guns B/156 followed close on the heels of the infantry and came into action on Western outskirts of village, and successfully engaged, over open sights, enemy Machine Guns. Infantry later, establihed themselves on eastern outskirts of CLARY, and immediately 2 guns B/156 were pushed through village and again came into action, shooting over open sights at 800 yards range, with extremely good effect. Infantry then pushed on through BERTRY, across railway and on to LA FAYTE and TROISVILLE, closely followed by 2 Guns each of "A" & B/156 who throughout the afternoon shot at very short ranges, in close support of Infantry, finally coming into action for the night, A/156 J.34.a cent., B/156 at J.36.c.9.1. Meanwhile the remainder of the Brigade was in close touch with the Infantry, and in the morning, from positions just west of CLARY, and in the afternoon, from positions just west of BERTRY, did excellent work, repeatedly engaging hostile movement, M.G's etc.	
	10th		At dawn the Infantry helped by Cavalry continued the advance, and made good the western bank of the River SELLE, the 156th Brigade pushing forward from BERTRY to positions in K.31 and K.32.	

(A9175) Wt W2358/P367 600,000 12/17 D. D. & L. Sch. 52a. Forms/C2118/15

to Sheet 3.

Army Form C. 2118.

WAR DIARY
or
INTELLIGENCE SUMMARY.
(Erase heading not required.)

Instructions regarding War Diaries and Intelligence Summaries are contained in F. S. Regs., Part II. and the Staff Manual respectively. Title pages will be prepared in manuscript.

Place	Date	Hour	Summary of Events and Information	Remarks and references to Appendices
	10th		Here excellent counter Battery work was carried out by D/156, who successfully engaged 4 hostile Batteries in action on forward slopes of high ground in K.10 and K.16.	
			Hostile Batteries, M.G's etc, were also engaged with good effect by remaining Batteries.	
		8 a.m.	' a.m. 10/10/18, Brigade located as under :-	
			H.Q/156- K.31.a.2.0.	
			A/156- K.25.d.2.9.	
			B/156- K.31.b.0.5.	
			C/156- K.31.a.6.2.	
			D/156- K.31.a.4.4.	
		5 p.m.	Fired barrage in support of unsuccessful attempt to capture high ground East of the SELLE.	
	12th	5 am.	100th Inf. Bde attacked without Artillery support, with objective high ground in K.18, K.11, and K.10, and despite strong opposition and enfilade M.G. fire, pushed on to-wards objectives. Strong counter attacks however forced infantry slowly back, and at about noon they had to with-draw to the western bank of the River.	
			During the early morning Artillery work was impossible, owing to mist, but later excellent work was done by all Batteries in silencing active M.G's, snipers, etc.	
	13/14th		Concentrations, and bombardments, of enemy strongpoints, M.G. nests etc.	
			Command of Artillery covering Divisional Front passed from C.R.A. 33rd Division to C.R.A. 38th Division.	
	15/16th		All Batteries carried out effective wirecutting, and harassing fire on enemy movement, M.G's etc.	
	17th	5.20am.	Fourth Army on our right, attacked. 156th Brigade R.F.A. fired in CHINESE Barrage, to cover left flank of 66th Division.	
	18th		Fired concentrations on RICHEMONT, CROISETTE, FOREST etc.	
	20th	7 am.	Fired barrage in support of attack by 38th Division, in conjunction with Third Army. Objectives high ground K.17, K.11, & K.5. Attack completely successful and at about 10.00 hrs Infantry reported all objectives gained.	
	21st		156th Brigade R.F.A. moved to positions N. of INCHY - LE CATEAU Road to cover OVILLERS SLAUGHTER HOUSE Road.	
			Adv. H.Q/156 - K.20.b.9.0.	
			A/156 - K.14.d.7.0.	
			B/156 - K.21.b.80.85.	
			C/156 - K.14.d.7.2.	
			D/156 - K.28.b.0.8.	

to Sheet 4.

(A9175) Wt W2358/P360 600,000 12/17 D. D. & L. Sch 52a. Forms/C2118/15

Instructions regarding War Diaries and Intelligence Summaries are contained in F. S. Regs., Part II. and the Staff Manual respectively. Title pages will be prepared in manuscript.

WAR DIARY
or
INTELLIGENCE SUMMARY.
(Erase heading not required.)

Army Form C. 2118.

Place	Date	Hour	Summary of Events and Information	Remarks and references to Appendices
	22nd		Reconnaissance of approaches and crossings of River SELLE carried out.	
	22/23		Command of Artillery covering Divisional Front passed from C.R.A. 38th Div to C.R.A. 33rd Div.	
	23rd	02.00	Under cover of a creeping barrage, 98th Inf. Bde continued the advance and at 04.30, 1st Middlesex were reported in FOREST, and 4th KINGS passing through, pushed on to next objective. At 05.30 B/156 with 1 section D/156 crossed the SELLE and reported to G.O.C. 98th Inf.Bde, afetr which, they followed up the leading Battalion, and throughout the day kept in close touch ~~with~~ with the advancing Infantry.	
			By 06.45 the remaining Batteries 156th Brigade R.F.A. had crossed the SELLE and were pushing on in close support, to positions in K.6 area.	
			At 09.00 the Brigade was located as follows :-	
			H.Q/156 - RICHEMONT.	
			A/156 - L.1.a.5.3.	
			B/156 - East of FOREST.	
			C/156 - K.5.c.7.4.	
		10.00	D/156 - K.6.b.4.0.	
			At 10.00, C/156 pushed on again and took up position at K.6.b.8.8.	
			Meanwhile the Infantry had pushed on, closely followed by B/156 and 1 Section D/156, and although meeting with strong opposition pushed on slowly through VENDEGIES WOOD. About 17.00 our front line was ~~apparently~~ approximately, Northern edge of VENDEGIES WOOD. Between 17.00 and 18.00, Batteries again moved forward and were located for night 23/24th as follows :-	
			H.Q/156 - K.6.b.8.8.	
			A/156 - L.1.a.0.1.	
			B/156 - F.26.b.50.85.	
			C/156 - F.25.a.3.8.	
			D/156 - F.25.a.6.6.	
			During the morning of 28th inst, whilst riding forward from RICHEMONT, Lt.Col.B.A.B.BUTLER, D.S.O.,R.F.A., was severely wounded, and died the same evening.	
			Major W.G.SHEERES,M.C., took over command of the Brigade.	
	24th	04.00	Heavy bursts of fire put down in front of Infantry, and under cover of this they commenced to push forward to-wards PAUL JACQUES FARM and WAGNONVILLE.	
			About 08.30 the Brigade moved forward, A/156 being in close support of the leading Battalion and at 09.00, the Brigade was in action in the VENDEGIES WOOD area :-	
			H.Q/156 - F.21.d.0.8.	
			B/156 - F.26.b.50.85.	
			C/156 - F.14.c.5.3.	
			D/156 - F.20.a.76.	

to sheet 5.

(A9175) Wt W2358/P360 600,000 12/17 D. D. & L.

Army Form C. 2118.

Instructions regarding War Diaries and Intelligence Summaries are contained in F. S. Regs., Part II. and the Staff Manual respectively. Title pages will be prepared in manuscript.

WAR DIARY
or
INTELLIGENCE SUMMARY.
(Erase heading not required.)

Place	Date	Hour	Summary of Events and Information	Remarks and references to Appendices
	24th		At after overcoming strong opposition the Infantry were reported through WAGNONVILLE and pushing on to-wards ENGLEFONTAINE. Positions were immediately reconnoitred in the WAGNONVILLE area and Batteries pushed on and came into action ad follows :- H.Q/156 - F.10.b.13. A/156 - F.11.a.2.8. B/156 - F.10.b.8.8. C/156 - F.4.c.23. D/156 - F.4.a.2.2. The Infantry being held up in the western outskirts of ENGLEFONTAINE.	
	26th	01.00	One Battalion from each of 98th and 19th I.B. attacked under thick Artillery barrage to complete capture of ENGLEFONTAINE. Attack completely successful, and some 500 prisoners and many M.Gs, were captured.	
	26/27th		33rd Division (less Artillery) relieved by 38th Division (less Artillery)	
	27th	05.50	Opened on S.O.S. lines in response to heavy hostile barrage, put down on ENGLEFONTAINE, small Infantry followed, in which 10 of our men were made prisoners.	
	28th		Following N.C.Os awarded Bar to M.M. 186876 Bdr W.G. COULT., B/156. 69311 Sgt A.C. WATMOUGH, C/156. Awarded M.M. 27923 Gnr E.MUNDAY, C/156. 6269 CplS/s A.T.MOORE, B/156. Lieut (A/Capt) Milnes K.W., appointed to Command A/156, Bde R.F.A., vice Capt (A/Major) F.B.H.CARRELL, struck off strength 18/10/18. 2/Lieut L.PESKIN, B/156 Bde R.F.A. appointed Second in Command B/156th Bde R.F.A. vice Lt(A/Major)S.G.TAYLOR,appointed to command A/162 Bde R.F.A. 2/10/1918.	
		19.30	D/156, fired gas concentration on hostile Battery, S.21.b.45, .	
	29th	01.30	A/156, fired gas concentration on S.28.a.77., and S.22.d.21 - 23.	
		08.00	156th Brigade R.F.A. fired creeping barrage in support of raid by 17th R.W.Fs on houses along ENGLEFONTAINE - BAVAI. Raid completely successful, about 70 prisoners taken and some 60 enemy killed.	
	30th		Lt(A/Major) K.W.MILNES, A/156 Bde R.F.A. awarded M.C.	
	31st	02.30	B/156 fired gas concentration on S.16.d.45. D/156 fired gas concentration on S.15.c.82 - S.15.d. 35. Brigade relieved in action by 169 A.F.A. Bde, and withdrew for 72 hours rest to billets in BERTRY.	

C G Sherey Maj
Cdg 156 Bgde RFA

(A9475) Wt W2358/P360 600,000 12/17 D. D. & L. Sch. 52a. Forms/C2118/15

27 156 Bde. R.F.A.

156th Brigade R.F.A.

Instructions regarding War Diaries and Intelligence Summaries are contained in F. S. Regs., Part II. and the Staff Manual respectively. Title pages will be prepared in manuscript.

WAR DIARY
or
INTELLIGENCE SUMMARY.
(Erase heading not required.)

Army Form C. 2118.

November 1918.

9/8 34

Place	Date	Hour	Summary of Events and Information	Remarks and references to Appendices
BERTRY	1st	0200	156th Bde R.F.A. marched into rest billets at BERTRY, having withdrawn from action near WAGNONVILLE for 72 hours rest, after handing over positions to 169 Army Brigade R.F.A.	
			No.19333 Corporal DAVEY.H.E, promoted to Sergeant by order of C.R.A. 33rd Division for gallantry in the Field.	
	2nd	1000	Positions reconniotred in F.3 and F.9 (near POIX DU NORD) to cover line S.26 central - A.2 central (East of ENGLEFONTAINE).	
Near POIX.		1500	Batteries marched out of BERTRY and came into action in new positions, and at 2000 hrs were located as follows:-	
			H.Q. F.4.c.1.6.	
			A. F.3.b.3.5.	
			B. F.3.d.1.6.	
			C. F.3.d.5.2.	
			D. F.4.d.25.90.	
			Lt.Col.C.E.BOYCE,D.S.O., took over command of the Brigade.	
	3rd		Close liaison between battalions and batteries maintained, and forward positions reconnoitred.	
	4th	0615	Brigade joined in creeping barrage fired in support of opening stages of attack by Vth Corps on MORMAL FOREST.	
		0810	All Batteries came off creeping barrage and began to move forward to positions East of ENGLEFONTAINE. The area allotted to the Brigade was being heavily Machine gunned and only A/156 was pushed forward. The remainder of the Brigade dropping temporarily into action West of the Village. Shortly after Machine Gun fire slackened and the remainder of the Brigade came forward, moves being so arranged that the whole of the Brigade front for creeping barrage was always covered.	
			At Noon, Brigade was located as under :-	
			H.Q. F.6.c.8.3 (with 114 Infantry Brigade).	
			A. A.8.a.3.7.	
			B. A.2.d.3.5.	
			C. A.2.d.3.8.	
			D. A.2.d.6.9.	
			From these positions barrage was continued until final protector was reached at about 1500 hrs. Positions were then reconnoitred in A.5 area, batteries moving forward at dusk. Great difficulty was experienced owing to roads being blown up and numerous trees felled across the roads, but by 2000 hrs batteries were all in action again.	
			H.Q. A.3.b.9.3 (with 100th Infantry Brigade).	
			A. A.5.c central.	
			B. A.10.b.8.3.	

(A9175) Wt W2358/P360 650,000 12/17 D. D. & L. Sch 52a. Forms/C2118/15

156th Brigade R.F.A.

Instructions regarding War Diaries and Intelligence Summaries are contained in F. S. Regs., Part II. and the Staff Manual respectively. Title pages will be prepared in manuscript.

November 1918.

Army Form C. 2118.

WAR DIARY
or
INTELLIGENCE SUMMARY.
(Erase heading not required.)

Place	Date	Hour	Summary of Events and Information	Remarks and references to Appendices
	4th		C. A.5.c central.	
			D. A.10.d.8.9.	
	5th	0400	Enemy were reported to have retired. One section per battery was immediately ordered forward and keep touch with battalions Commanders. These advanced through LA GRANDE PATURES and took up positions East of SARBARAS, which gave easy command of the crossings to and the ground beyond the River SAMBRE. Successful observed fire was carried out, and much enemy movement engaged.	
			Meanwhile the remaining guns of the Brigade were hurried forward, but great delay was caused by congestion on roads, mine craters etc.	
			At noon Brigade was in action complete, located as under:-	
			H.Q. T.30.c.5.0.	
			A. C.2.a.6.3.	
			B. C.1.d.52.78.	
			C, C.1.c.85.80.	
			D. B.6.d.10.55.	
			During afternoon reconnaissances of routes forward and crossings of River SAMBRE carried out.	
	6th		Enemy withdrew to East of SAMBRE and were followed up by 162 & 169 Brigades R.F.A. 156th Brigade remaining in position West of the River.	
	7th		B/156 moved to U.26.b.40.85.	
		1700	Wagons sent across SAMBRE to help establish advanced A.R.P. at C.6.b.5.0.	
	8/11th		Men were comfortably billetted and time spent in generally cleaning up.	
	11th	1100	Hostilities ceased.	
	11/13th		Cleaning up continued.	
	14th		Brigade marched to VENDEGIES + CROIX area via RIBAUMET - BERLIAMONT - ENGLEFONTAINE.	
	15th		Brigade marched to CLARY - MONTIGNY area via NEUVILLY - INCHY and AUDENCOURT.	
	16th		Brigade marched to CREVECOEUR area via ESNES and LESDAIN.	
	19th		Brigade marched to VILLERS OUTREAUX.	
	22nd		Thanksgiving Service.	
	23rd		Lieut.Colonel C.E.BOYCE,D.S.O., proceeded on leave to ENGLAND. Major D.E.JONES,M.C. takes over command of Brigade.	
	17/30th		Overhauling and cleaning equipment. Salvage work.	
			Afternoons and evenings devoted to games and general recreation.	
			AWARDS :- Major W.G. SHEERES awarded bar to M.C.	
			Captain.L.PESKIN awarded M.C.	
			B.S.M. MARSHALL.D. D/156 awarded Military Medal.	

D.E. Jones
Major R.F.A.
Commanding 156th Brigade R.F.A.

(A9175) Wt W2358/P360 600,000 12/17 D. D. & L. Sch 52a. Forms/C2118/15

Instructions regarding War Diaries and Intelligence Summaries are contained in F. S. Regs., Part II. and the Staff Manual respectively. Title pages will be prepared in manuscript.

Army Form C. 2118.

WAR DIARY of 156th Brigade RFA
or INTELLIGENCE SUMMARY.

(Erase heading not required.)

1/31 December 1918

Vol 35

Place	Date	Hour	Summary of Events and Information	Remarks and references to Appendices
1/6 Dec 1918			At Villers Outreaux - time spent on cleaning & general overhaul of equipment, salvage etc	
6.			Bde had orders to move and marched to TINCOURT, where the night was spent	
7			Marched to RIENCOURT	
8			" " BLANGY-TRONVILLE	
9			" " LE MESGE	
10			" " SELINCOURT and DROMESNIL where Bde halted for 2 days. ~~Time spent~~	
11/12			At Selincourt & Dromesnil, time spent cleaning vehicles & harness.	
13			Marched to BROCOURT-LIOMER where Bde are now in billets	
14/21			General overhaul of vehicles & equipment, slightly hampered by inclement weather.	
22/24			These days were spent in making preparations for the entertainment of the men during Xmas.	
25/26			Xmas festivities	
27/31			General training including route-marching. Educational classes were held during the mornings and the afternoons were generally spent in recreational physical training. Concerts & lectures were given to the men during the evenings.	
31.			Major General Sir Reginald Pinney, KCB, visited the Bde at 14:45 hrs & presented ribands to certain Officers & O.Rs.	

E [illegible] Lieut Col RFA
Comdg 156th Bde RFA

(A9175) Wt W2358/P360 600,000 12/17 D. D. & L. Sch. 52a. Forms/C2118/15

January 1919.

WAR DIARY.

Army Form C.2118.

156th Brigade R.F.A.

33rd

Place	Date	Hour	Summary of Events and Information.	Remarks and references to Appendices.
BROCOURT	11th		2/Lieut.W.R.F.FISHER, B/156 proceeded home for demobilization.	36
	18th		2/Lieut.C.P.HANKINS, A/156 proceeded home for demobilization.	
	19th		" W.H.SNELL, B/156 proceeded home for demobilization.	
	25th		Major General WARDROP, G.O.C., R.A., Third Army, inspected the Brigade.	
	27th		Inspection of vehicles, Gun Park Stores etc, by C.R.A., 33rd Division.	
	28th		Lieut.H.V.CUSHING., A/156 proceeded home for demobilization.	
	29th		Lieut.P.R.M.HANNA., C/156 proceeded home for demobilization.	
	30th		100 "Z" animals left the Brigade for No. 7 Veterinary Hospital.	

HONOURS & AWARDS

No. 52330 Fitter Staff Sergt.W.J.RUSSELL, H.Q/156 awarded M.S.M.
No. 253797 Sapper H.LAMPARD, 33rd Div.Sig.Coy, R.E., Attd HQ/156 Bde R.F.A. awarded M.S.M.
No. 82506 Sergt. W.S.SAINSBURY, D/156 awarded D.C.M.
No. 52363 B.S.M. D.MARSHALL, D/156 awarded D.C.M.

[signature] Major R.F.A.
Commanding 156th Brigade R.F.A.

17

A.F.C.2118.

WAR DIARY

156 Bde RFA

February 1919

156th Brigadec R.F.A.

33rd

Place	Date	Hour	Summary of Events and Information	Remarks & references to appendice
BROCOURT.	1/25th		On Lines of Communication.	
	25th.		Lieut.D.CAIRD, proceeded home for demobilization. Lieut. G.H.GOODERHAM, C/156 preceeded to England for Repatriation to Canada.	
	28th		Lieut-Colonel C.E.BOYCE.,D.S.O., proceeded to England to take up War Office Appointment.	

Major R.F.A.
Commanding 156th Brigade R.F.A.

War Diary.

March 1919. | 156th Brigade R.F.A.

33

Vol 38

Place	Date	Hour	Summary of Events & Information.
BRECOURT	1st.		On Lines of Communication.
	7th		Capt. G. Fleming, B/156 proceeded to England for Demobilization & repatriation to AUSTRALIA
	10th		Major V. Bennet-Stanford, C/156, proceeded to England for duty in India & Mesopotamia
	12th		Lt. E. Morris, B/156, proceeded to England for duty in India & Mesopotamia.
	13th		Major S. G. Taylor, posted to B/156 from A/162 Bde R.F.A.
	14th		Lt. F. E. S. Groves, proceeded to England for duty in India & Mesopotamia.

[signature] Capt. for Major RFA
Commanding 156 Bde RFA.

War Diary

April 1919 — 156th Brigade RFA

Place	Date	Hour	Summary of Events & Information
Brocourt	1st	-	2/Lt A A KENNINGHAM left for BEAUCAMPS for Army of Occupation personnel.
Blangy-sur-Bresle	2nd	-	The Brigade left BROCOURT and concentrated at BLANGY-SUR-BRESLE
	3rd	-	All animals of the Brigade loaned to other Brigades.
	4th		Major D. E. JONES M.C, Capt. W. G. PRINGLE, and 2/Lt CORRIE left the Brigade for Army of Occupation. Major S. G. TAYLOR assumed command of the Brigade.
	6th	-	45 Animals proceeded to Remount Depot Abbeville.
	24th	-	All R.E. personnel of this Brigade proceeded to ETRETAT to rejoin 33rd Div. Signal Company R.E.
	28th		Lieut J. PICKEN 1st Queens Own Royal Glasgow Yeomanry, Horse Adviser attached to this Brigade proceeded to Concentration Camp Abbeville for Demobilization.

S G Taylor
Major RFA
Commanding 156 Brigade RFA

33 DIVISIONAL ARTILLERY

156 BRIGADE R.F.ARTILLERY.

MAY 1919 MISSING

156th Brigade R.F.A.

156 Bde R.F.A.

Instructions regarding War Diaries and Intelligence Summaries are contained in F. S. Regs., Part II, and the Staff Manual respectively. Title pages will be prepared in manuscript.

WAR DIARY
or
INTELLIGENCE SUMMARY.
(Erase heading not required.)

Army Form C. 2118.

June 1919.

VS 41

ceased

Place	Date	Hour	Summary of Events and Information	Remarks and references to Appendices
Blangy [illegible]	1st		Brigade stationed at CHINK CAMP Blangy.	
	9th		The Cadres of HQ. A+D Batteries proceeded to UK for dispersal. leaving an Equipment Guard of 1 Officer + [illegible] men for HQ and 1 Officer and 15 men per Battery. Capt H.W. Smart + 2/Lt [illegible] [illegible] proceeded with Cadre.	
	13th		The Cadres of B+C Batteries proceeded to UK for dispersal. leaving an Equipment Guard of 15 men per Battery. Major S.G. Taylor + Capt L. [illegible] proceeded with Cadre.	
	11th		~~Equipment Guards of HQ B+D Batteries entrained at Blangy for Le Havre.~~	
	21st		~~Equipment Guards of A+C Batteries entrained at Blangy for LE HAVRE.~~	

A.H.H. Spencer Lt
for Capt R.F.A.
Comdg 156 Bde [illegible] R.F.A.

D. D. & L., London, E.C.
(A7883) Wt. W809/M1672 350,000 4/17 Sch. 52a Forms/C/2118/14

www.ingramcontent.com/pod-product-compliance
Lightning Source LLC
Chambersburg PA
CBHW081526160426
43191CB00011B/1696